Cleveland in 50 Maps

Cleveland in 50 Maps

Edited by Dan Crissman
Cartography by Evan Tachovsky and David Wilson

Belt Publishing
Cleveland, OH

Printed in the United States of America
First edition, 2019
ISBN: 978-1-948742-55-9

Belt Publishing
3143 West 33rd Street, #6
Cleveland, Ohio 44109
www.beltpublishing.com

Cover art and book design by David Wilson
Cartography by Evan Tachovsky

"Ordinary life is pretty complex stuff."
—Harvey Pekar

TABLE OF CONTENTS

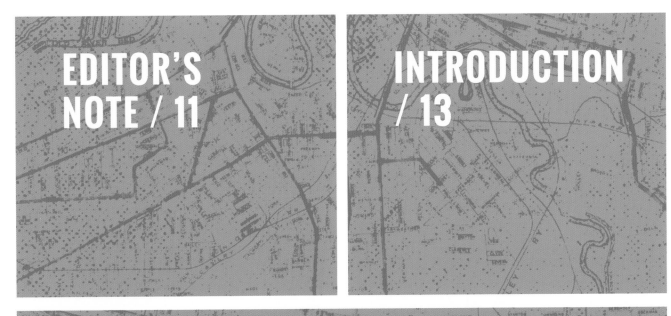

SECTION TWO

GETTING AROUND
THE CITY / 35

SECTION THREE

COMMUNITIES OF
CLEVELANDERS / 51

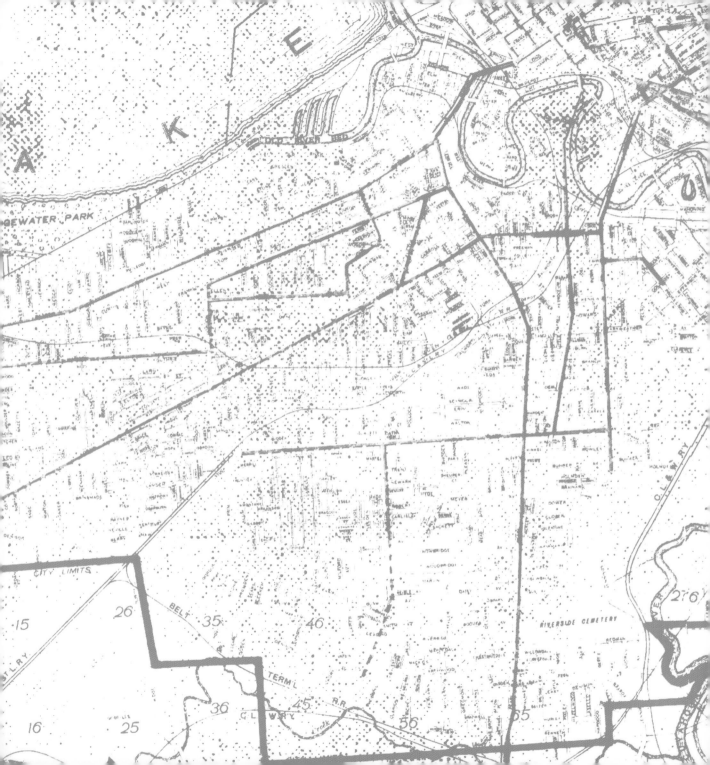

Before you dive in and begin answering questions about Cleveland you never thought to ask, I should preface with a disclaimer: The title of this book should really be *Cleveland in (About) 50 Maps*. Depending on what you count as "one" map, there are as many as 65 in the pages that follow, exploring the history, topography, demographics, industry, politics, and culture of this great Midwestern city. But 50 is a nice round number, so we're going with that.

One other very important thing to mention is that what you are about to read could not have been possible without the hard work, creativity, and technological know-how of the team at Belt Publishing. Thanks go out to David Wilson and Anne Trubek for their amazing work on this project.

There's one person, however, without whom this book simply would not exist: Evan Tachovsky. In addition to compiling all the data, Evan was the brilliant mind and animating force behind the conception and execution of each map. While he now lives in New York City, Evan's love for his hometown helped make this book what it is, and all of us at Belt are truly thankful.

—Dan Crissman

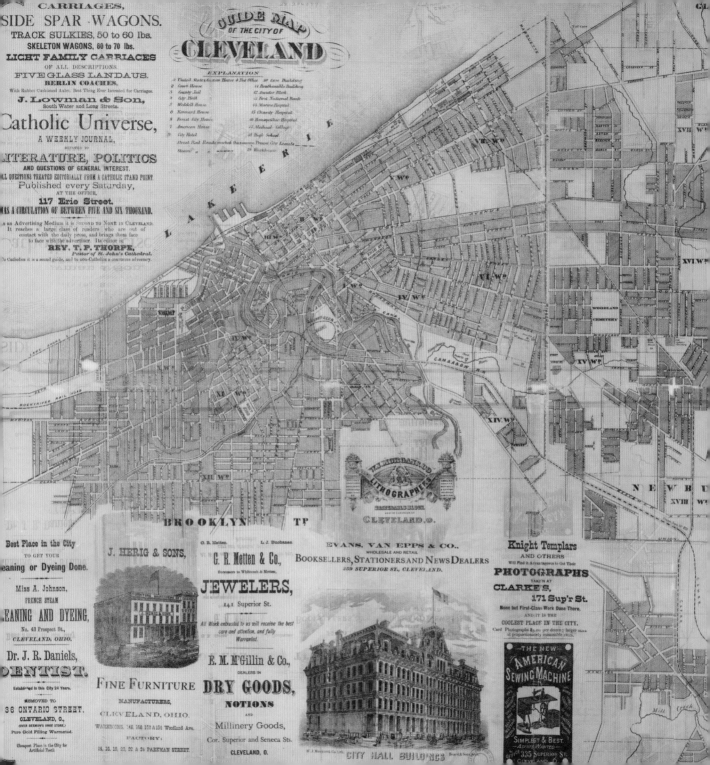

GUIDE MAP OF THE CITY OF CLEVELAND

EXPLANATION

1 United States Custom House & Post Office.
2 Court House
3 County Jail
4 City Hall
5 Weddell House
6 Kennard House
7 Forest City House
8 American House
9 City Hotel
10 Case Building
11 Brotherhood's Building
12 Atwater Block
13 First National Bank
14 Marine Hospital
15 Charity Hospital
16 Homœopathic Hospital
17 Medical College
18 High School
19 Workhouse
Street Rail Roads marked thus ——— Present City Limits
Steam " " ———

LAKE ERIE

BROOKLYN   T P

INTRODUCTION

What can a map tell you about a city? Almost anything you want to know.

If you're just trying to get from Point A to Point B, maps can help you figure out the best route. If you're a tourist exploring a new area, maps can highlight must-see attractions and the best spots to eat and drink. If you want to know about a particular population, maps can tell you all sorts of things about who a city's residents are, where they're from, how long they've been there, and what they're lives might be like. If you're interested in understanding the history of a particular place, maps can shed light on what its environs used to look like, or allow you to see the future that its leaders envisioned in the past. Likewise, if you want to predict a city's future, maps can show you the trends and plans that will help shape it.

This book was inspired by that idea. We wanted to use 50 (or so) maps to tell the story of a city we love: Cleveland, Ohio. Together, they would convey not just who and what comprises a city, but how it feels to be there.

Cleveland is a fascinating place. (No, seriously.) The easternmost city in the Midwest, Cleveland sits at the mouth of a narrow, crooked river that empties into the shallowest of the Great Lakes. It can trace its European settlement history back to the eighteenth century and its Native settlement history many centuries farther. Once, it was one of the five most populous cities in the United States, but now it no longer even cracks the top fifty. It has long been a haven to dozens of ethnic communities from around the globe, yet it remains one of the most segregated cities in America. It is a beleaguered sports town that now proudly claims the title of City of Champions (if somewhat ironically). It is the birthplace of Superman, the Polish Boy, and rock and roll.

Guide Map of the City of Cleveland, 1877 (Courtesy of the Cleveland Public Library Map Collection)

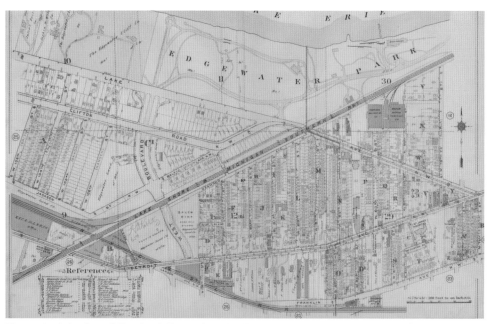

Plat Book of the City of Cleveland, Ohio, Volume 2, Plate 24, G. M. Hopkins & Co., 1912 (Courtesy of the Cleveland Public Library Map Collection)

(previous page) Cleveland Picture Map, 1928 (Courtesy of the Cleveland Public Library Map Collection)

The maps in the following pages are broken up into five different sections. The first section, "The Lay of the Land," explores the physical features of the city. You'll see how the borders expanded over time; how elevation, waterways, and tree coverage shaped our surroundings; and the Metroparks system conserves our natural landscape.

The second section, "Getting Around the City," maps the idiosyncratic infrastructure that dots the region. You'll find maps showing how bridges, highways, parking lots, and rail lines help—and hinder—the flow of traffic between neighborhoods. You'll discover the most walkable sections of the city and perhaps finally understand the method behind the naming of streets, avenues, roads, and boulevards.

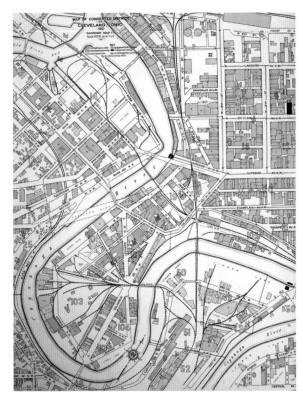

Map of Congested District of Cleveland, Ohio, Sanborn Map Company, 1912 (Courtesy of the Cleveland Public Library Map Collection)

The third section, "Communities of Clevelanders," dives into the demographic makeup of the city, mapping citizens by age, ethnicity, socioeconomic status, and other factors. Of particular interest is the map on page 60, showing in stark terms the effects of the federally sanctioned redlining policies in the twentieth century. You'll see clearly how the lines in this map are mirrored in countless others throughout the book.

The fourth section, spotlighting the city's various institutions, is perhaps the most fun. Compare the number of breweries in the city before Prohibition and today. Explore the vast salt mine under Lake Erie, and track the expansion of the Cleveland Clinic. Relive the championship parade and the breathless campaign stops of 2016. See which Cleveland businesses were featured in the famous *Green Book*, and follow the movements of the city's most popular music venues.

The final section, "Looking Ahead," projects the changes coming to Cleveland in the near future. See what the various planned "opportunity zones" and "opportunity corridors" could mean for your community—and how you can get involved in writing the city's next chapter.

CLEVELAND IN 1830

CLEVELAND IN 1860

CLEVELAND IN 1890

CLEVELAND IN 1920

Historians are unsure if the site that was to become the city of Cleveland was inhabited or not when Moses Cleaveland arrived in 1796. What is clear, however, is that Cleaveland, a general in the Connecticut Land Company, decided it should be the new capital of Connecticut's Western Reserve—regardless of what Native peoples might already live there. He laid plans for a city, taking advantage of the natural geography that would make it a great trading post for the territory. Then Cleaveland promptly went back to his home in Connecticut, never to return.

A few white settlers stayed, and by 1814 they incorporated the village of Cleaveland, which became Cleveland when a newspaper lacked room on the masthead for the additional "a". In 1820, the population of Cleveland was 606; the completion of the Ohio and Erie Canal in 1832 made Cleveland an important port on the Great Lakes, and the city grew, especially around the banks of the rivers and lake.

At the time, Ohio City was a separate settlement on the other side of the river from Cleveland. In 1836, when Cleveland built the Columbus Bridge, connecting the two cities, the citizens of Ohio City were incensed. They rallied for "Two Bridges or None!" and bombed and vandalized the bridge, climaxing in a battle upon the bridge that wounded two men. By 1854, the antagonism between the two cities had subsided, and Cleveland officially annexed Ohio City.

By 1860 the population of the city had grown to 43,417. After the Civil War, the city became a shipping hub for iron ore from the west, coal from the south, and the rise of manufacturing, particularly steel. Bessamer Steel first "blew" in 1868, when the city was one of the five largest oil refining centers in the country. In 1870, John D. Rockefeller founded Standard Oil, and the population of the city doubled to 92,829, becoming the fifteenth largest city in the nation.

The boom continued, and by 1920, Cleveland was the fifth largest city in the United States, with 796,841 people, a growth achieved in part by its earlier annexation of many nearby villages, including Glenville and South Brooklyn in 1905, Corlett Village in 1909, Collinwood in 1910, and Nottingham in 1912, and portions of other cities along the east and west borders.

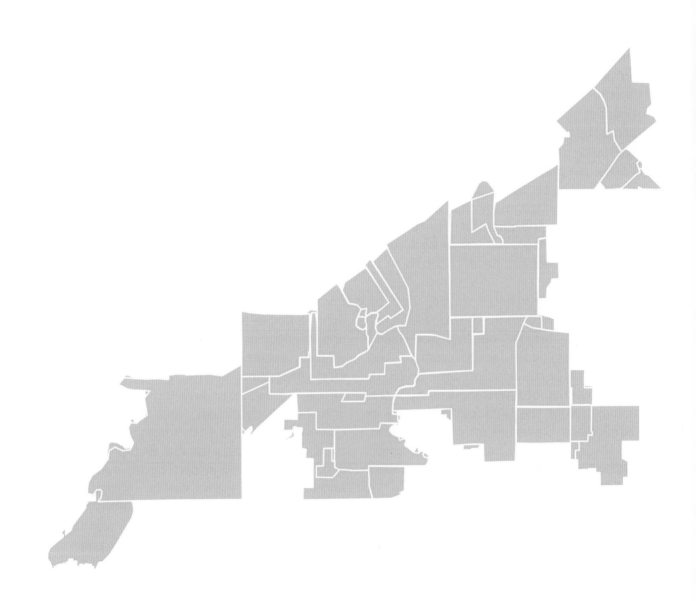

CLEVELAND TODAY

Today, the city of Cleveland encompasses over 82 square miles. Thirty distinct neighborhoods, from Collinwood to Kamm's Corners, lie within its borders. It is the seat of Cuyahoga County, which includes the inner-ring suburbs of Parma, Lakewood, Euclid, Cleveland Heights, and Shaker Heights, among others.

Overall, Cleveland's population has fallen from its midcentury heights to a more modest 383,793, according to the latest US Census Bureau estimates. That's about a 10,000-person decline even from the last official count, conducted in 2010, putting Cleveland fifty-second on the list of the largest cities in the United States. The Greater Cleveland metropolitan area is currently home to more than two million residents, the thirty-second biggest metro region in the nation.

Though population numbers are trending downward, Cleveland may continue to grow in area, at least. The borders of the city have remained fairly stable since the 1940s, when the area that became Hopkins Airport was ceded from the town of Brook Park. The last annexation came in August 2001, when Cleveland and Brook Park agreed to redraw their official borders around the I-X Center. In 2016, the financially distressed city of East Cleveland passed legislation approving a merger with neighboring Cleveland, though negotiations between the two city councils subsequently fell apart.

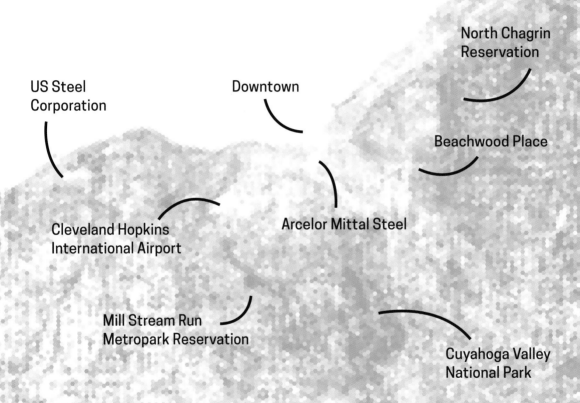

Darker color indicates more trees

US Steel
Corporation

Downtown

North Chagrin
Reservation

Beachwood Place

Cleveland Hopkins
International Airport

Arcelor Mittal Steel

Mill Stream Run
Metropark Reservation

Cuyahoga Valley
National Park

TREE COVERAGE IN NORTHEAST OHIO

It may come as a surprise to those not from Cleveland (or even to those who've spent their whole lives here) that Cleveland's official nickname is "The Forest City." But when you look around, it is impossible not to see why. The iconic images of Cleveland may be oversized barges and burning rivers, but trees are a far more common sight—especially when you venture further from downtown.

If you look closely at this map, what stand out are the areas without significant tree cover. Downtown, Hopkins Airport, and the steel mills are of course nearly treeless, but they are the exception not the rule. The dark half circle in the middle of this map—from the Mill Stream Run into the Cuyahoga Valley National Park and up northeastward towards the North Chagrin Reservation—forms a chain of nature reservations maintained by the Cleveland Metroparks System. (See page 32 for more on the Cleveland Metroparks System.) Even one of the largest malls in the area, Beachwood Place, sits on the doorstep of a reservation dedicated to preserving the natural landscape.

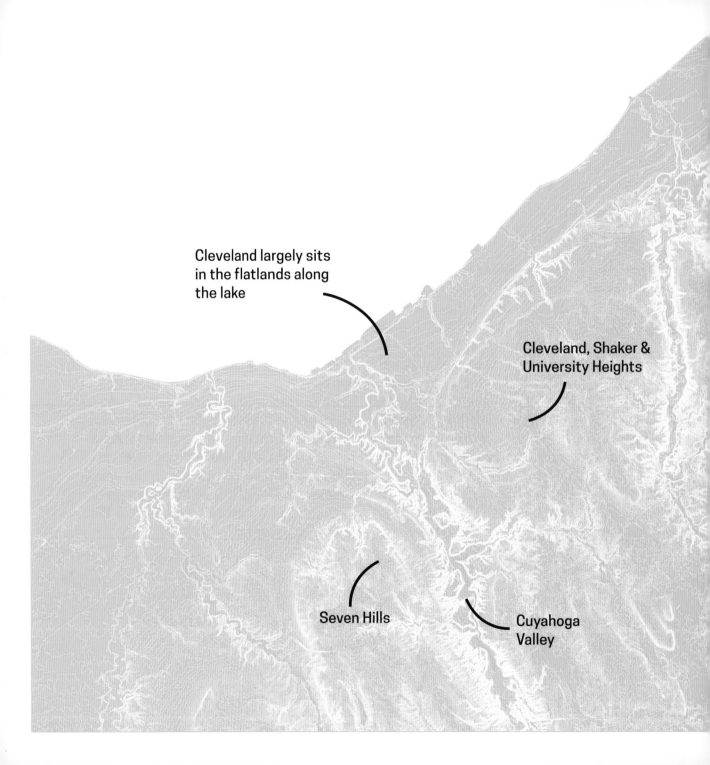

Cleveland largely sits in the flatlands along the lake

Cleveland, Shaker & University Heights

Seven Hills

Cuyahoga Valley

ELEVATION

Most outsiders think of Ohio as the beginning of America's breadbasket, filled with flat rolling cornfields and big sky. But the same glaciers that carved out Lake Erie shaped Northeast Ohio as well, and you can still see the scars they left in the landscape.

Much of the city sits in the flatlands along the lake, including the tragic misuse of prime waterfront land that is Burke Airport. The lowest points in the city, called "the Flats," follow the east and west banks of the Cuyahoga. Downtown, Ohio City, and Tremont sit on small plateaus leading up from the Flats.

Perched above the city to the southeast are some of the city's earliest suburbs, atop a plateau known affectionately as "the Heights." Many of these towns have naturally adopted the moniker as a signifier—Cleveland Heights, University Heights, Mayfield Heights, Richmond Heights, Maple Heights, Warrensville Heights, and, of course, Shaker Heights. (For more on Shaker Heights, check out pages 66-69.)

To the south, Cuyahoga Valley National Park offers some of the region's best hiking, including the Ledges Trail and Tinker's Gorge. The area directly to the west of the park is known for its hilly terrain, including the aptly named suburb of Seven Hills.

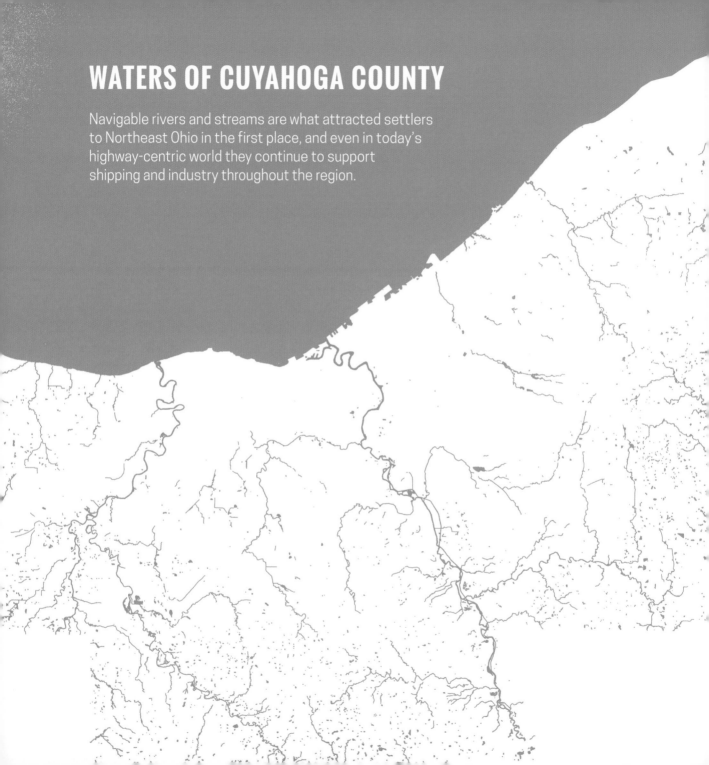

WATERS OF CUYAHOGA COUNTY

Navigable rivers and streams are what attracted settlers to Northeast Ohio in the first place, and even in today's highway-centric world they continue to support shipping and industry throughout the region.

MAJOR RIVERS

Given the crooked paths and shallow beds of the Cuyahoga, Rocky, and Chagrin Rivers, it's amazing they are navigable at all. Pass an afternoon on the banks of the Cuyahoga in downtown Cleveland and you're likely to see barges like the 634-foot MV *Buffalo* slowly inching their way down river, trying desperately not to run aground.

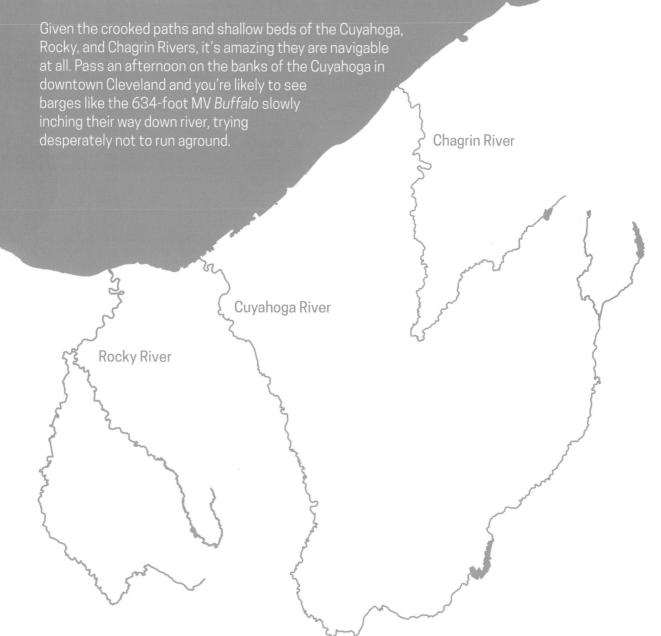

Chagrin River

Cuyahoga River

Rocky River

FLOOD ZONES

With increased precipitation from climate change comes new flood zones, and requirements for flood insurance in high-risk areas. In 2011, the US government revised the flood plain map for the county, increasing the areas considered high-risk.

Homeowners living in federally designated flood zones are required to purchase flood insurance, which is expensive, running from $125 to over $6,000 per year, as well as raising all insurance premiums and potentially lowering property values.

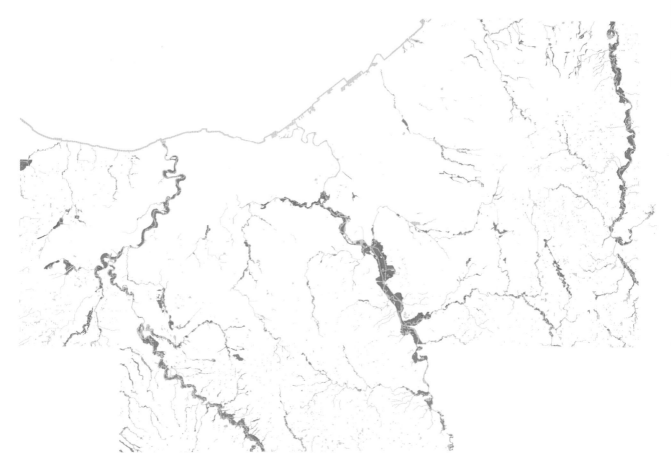

LAKE ERIE ICE COVERAGE

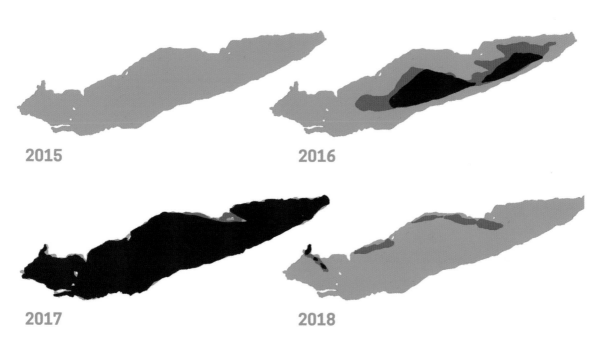

2015

2016

2017

2018

The amount of ice covering Lake Erie fluctuates year to year, but the overall trend is sharply downward: between 1973-2010, the amount of ice cover on Lake Erie has declined 50%. Sharp fluctuations, such as that seen in the "polar vortex" year of 2017 shown here, are due to normal extreme weather patterns as well as man-made climate change. Reduced ice coverage benefits the multi-billion dollar shipping industry, increases lake effect snow, lowers water levels in summers, and harms local ecosystems.

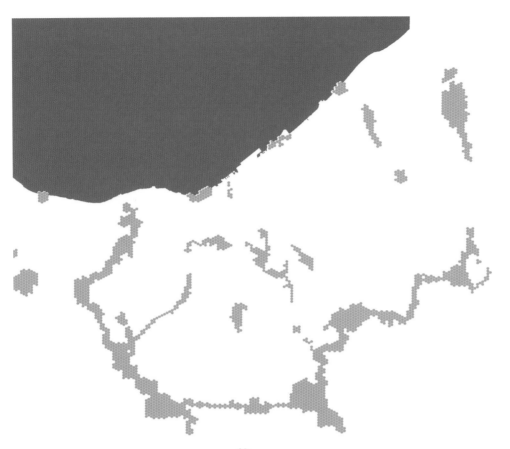

CLEVELAND METROPARKS

The Cleveland Metroparks system is one of the Forest City's jewels. With over 23,000 acres encircling the region (hence the name "Emerald Necklace"), the major parks of the Metroparks system are not planned green spaces, à la Central Park in New York or the Boston Commons. Many are instead wildlife preserves or natural landscapes with hundreds of miles of trails, picnic areas, and community centers.

CLEVELAND METROPARKS
SIZED BY VISITOR OCCASIONS / SQ FOOT

Admission is free for nearly all the parks during daylight hours. Despite a roughly even distribution in acreage between the east and west sides, however, the areas bordering the lakefront as well as the Rocky River and Big Creek Reservations receive the vast proportion of visitors.

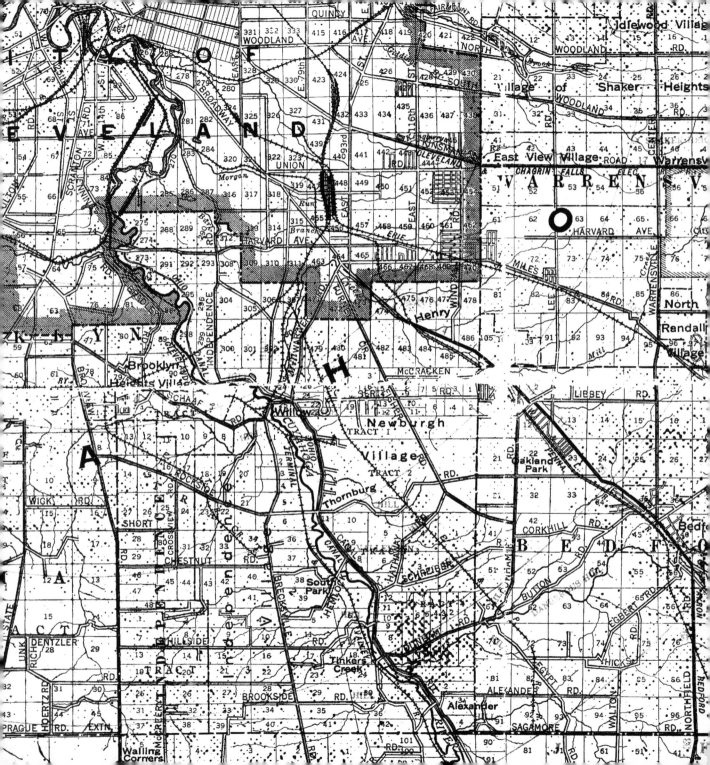

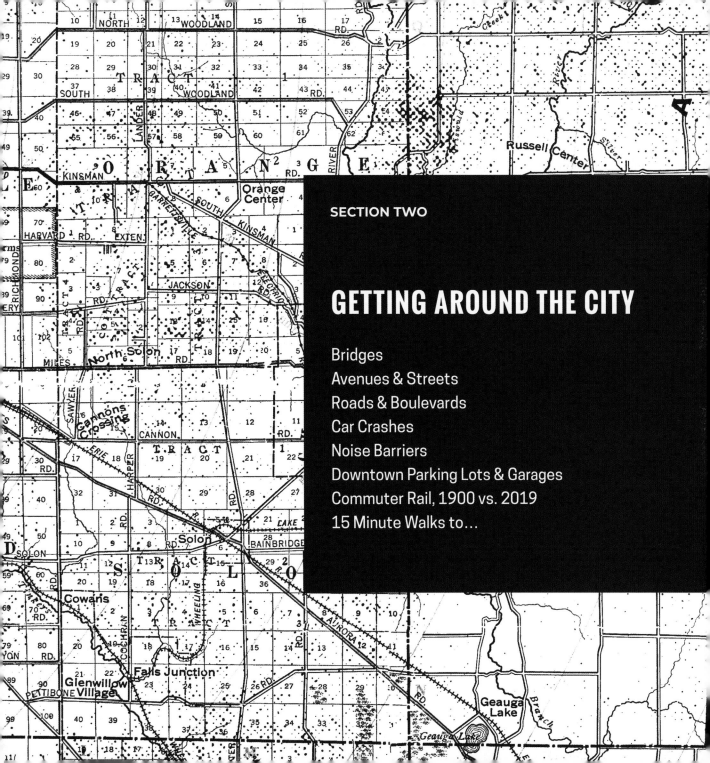

SECTION TWO

GETTING AROUND THE CITY

Bridges
Avenues & Streets
Roads & Boulevards
Car Crashes
Noise Barriers
Downtown Parking Lots & Garages
Commuter Rail, 1900 vs. 2019
15 Minute Walks to…

BRIDGES **OF CLEVELAND**

The Cuyahoga River cuts its way through the city like a cleaver, carving a deep valley from its mouth at Lake Erie miles south through the Cuyahoga Valley National Park. It is the demarking line between the East Side and the West Side of town and crossing it, especially near the heart of downtown Cleveland, has been a challenge since the earliest settlers arrived on its banks. The dozens of bridges constructed across the water look like a M.C. Escher piece at first glance, multiple constructions of different materials, angles, and elevations. The major bridges include:

① First Flats Rail Bridge
Now unimaginatively known as Cuyahoga River Bridge #1, this rail-only lift crossing, constructed in 1954, is the last before the Cuyahoga empties into Lake Erie.

② Main Avenue Viaduct
Built in 1938, this cantilever truss bridge hovers above the Flats, carrying drivers along the Route 2 highway.

③ Detroit-Superior Bridge
Also known as the Veterans Memorial Bridge, this through-type arch bridge links Public Square to Detroit Avenue.

④ Hope Memorial Bridge
Famous for its 40-foot tall art-deco "Guardians of Transportation" statues, this 1927 bridge connects Ohio City with Tribe fans' beloved corner of Carnegie and Ontario.

⑤ George V. Voinovich Bridges
The two recently renovated I-90 connectors offer an ever-changing light display on their undersides each night.

The riverside is also dotted with many rusted steel bridges no longer safe to walk upon, except for the bravest of ill-advised teenagers, as well as modern additions, as always, under construction.

AVENUES **OF CLEVELAND**

Given the cockeyed angle of the city, it's hard to envision a grid in the traditional sense of city planning. But there is a method to the seeming madness. All avenues, for example, run east to west.

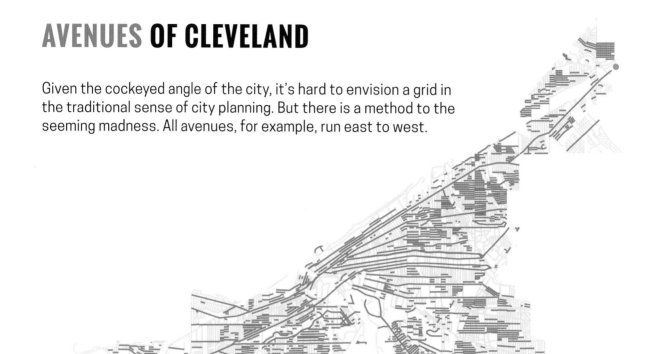

STREETS **OF CLEVELAND**

Similarly, all streets in the city run north to south.

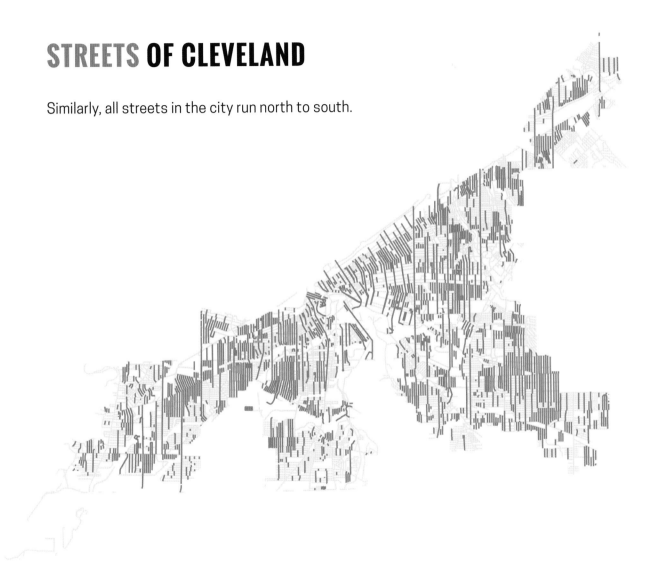

ROADS **OF CLEVELAND**

Roads tend to run diagonally, linking common
commuter destinations.

BOULEVARDS **OF CLEVELAND**

Boulevards are mainly scenic routes, often following the natural contours of the landscape.

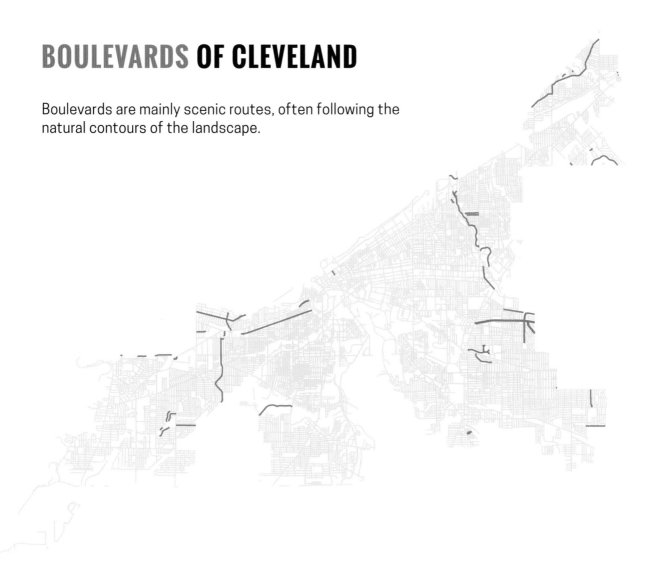

CAR ACCIDENTS IN 2018

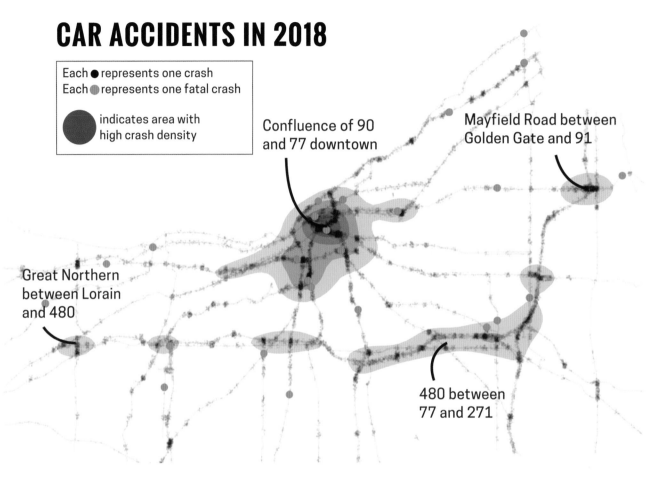

Each ● represents one crash
Each ◗ represents one fatal crash

⬤ indicates area with high crash density

Confluence of 90 and 77 downtown

Mayfield Road between Golden Gate and 91

Great Northern between Lorain and 480

480 between 77 and 271

Like any city, Cleveland's interstate highways can clog up at high-traffic areas during rush hour, which inevitably leads to accidents. As you can see in the map above, places where major routes merge are disproportionately likely to be the site of crashes, including fatal ones. One surprise, though, is that the sharp turn where I-90 meets Route 2 just east of downtown—dubbed Dead Man's Curve—actually appears far safer than the meeting of I-90 and I-77 by Progressive Field.

NOISE BARRIERS IN CUYAHOGA COUNTY

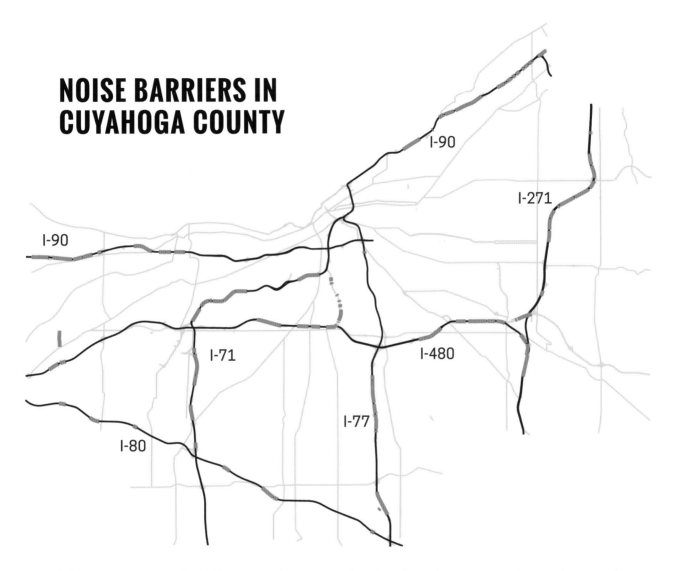

I-90

I-90

I-271

I-71

I-480

I-77

I-80

Highways are an undeniably convenient way to get around, but they come at a cost for the areas they snake through. To mitigate the constant hum of cars whizzing by, large barriers have been erected around some of the city's busiest stretches, often cutting off neighboring communities from each other while doing little to block the noise.

PARKING LOTS **OF CLEVELAND**

When the city planners of Cleveland laid out the downtown grid, leaving ample space for parking cars was not a consideration. But to accommodate an increasingly sprawling suburban population, city leaders in the twentieth century cleared as much space as they could wrest away for paved lots.

Looking at this map, though, many Cleveland residents may be surprised that there isn't more acreage dedicated to parking, especially considering just how many lots and garages dot the heart of downtown by the sports arenas. Indeed, one of downtown's hottest draws—the restaurants and bars of pedestrian-friendly East 4th Street, featuring fine dining options such as Michael Symon's Lola and Jonathon Sawyer's Greenhouse Tavern—overlooks a sea of blacktop flanked by stories-tall garages on three sides.

One parking lot residents hold more affection for is the Muni-Lot, which is something of a Cleveland institution. Located within eyesight of the lakeshore and tucked ungracefully between an embankment and I-90, the Muni-Lot is the site of the more infamous tailgate for the Cleveland Browns games each Sunday in the fall. It can be seen on the map stretching along the shoreline just south of Burke Airport.

■1900   ■2019

CLEVELAND COMMUTER RAIL

At the turn of the twentieth century, like many cities in the Midwest, Cleveland had an extensive streetcar network. Trains and trolleys were the dominant method of transportation from the city's many far-flung neighborhoods and inner-ring suburbs into the heart of downtown. You could board a streetcar in Rocky River and be able to exit in Old Brooklyn, or get on in Garfield Heights and end up in Glenville.

The first streetcar was built in 1859, connecting East 55th Street with downtown. Three suburban steam lines followed over the next two decades, and in the 1890s the system was consolidated and electrified. At one point, the city of Cleveland had over 400 miles of streetcar lines.

Unfortunately, also like many other Midwestern cities, this network was largely dismantled by the mid-twentieth century to make way for interstate highways and the rising culture of dependency on personal vehicles. When the Greater Cleveland Rapid Transit Authority (GCRTA) was formed at the end of 1974, the agency assumed control over the Shaker Heights light rail lines operated by the Van Swearingen brothers. In 1978, the two lines were rechristened the Blue and Green Lines and joined with Cleveland's Red Line. Though to this day, for inexplicable reasons, there is no free transfer between these separate lines.

WHO LIVES IN WITHIN 15 MINUTES WALKING TIME FROM A CLEVELAND PUBLIC LIBRARY BRANCH?

WHO LIVES IN WITHIN 15 MINUTES WALKING TIME FROM A THEATER?

WHO LIVES IN WITHIN 15 MINUTES WALKING TIME FROM A SUPERMARKET?

WHO LIVES IN WITHIN 15 MINUTES WALKING TIME FROM A FARMERS MARKET?

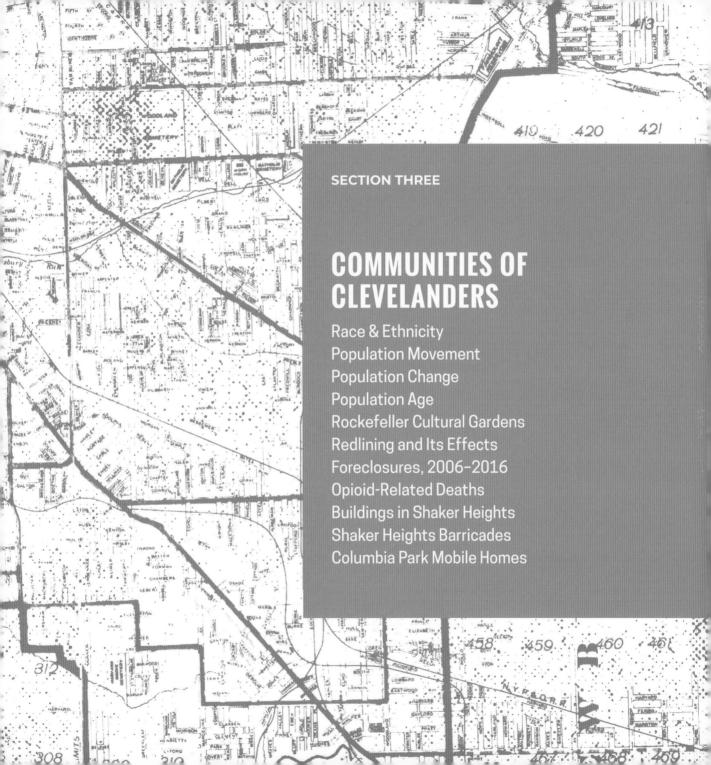

COMMUNITIES OF CLEVELANDERS

RACE & ETHNICITY IN CUYAHOGA COUNTY

Each dot = 50 People

- White
- African American
- Latino
- Asian

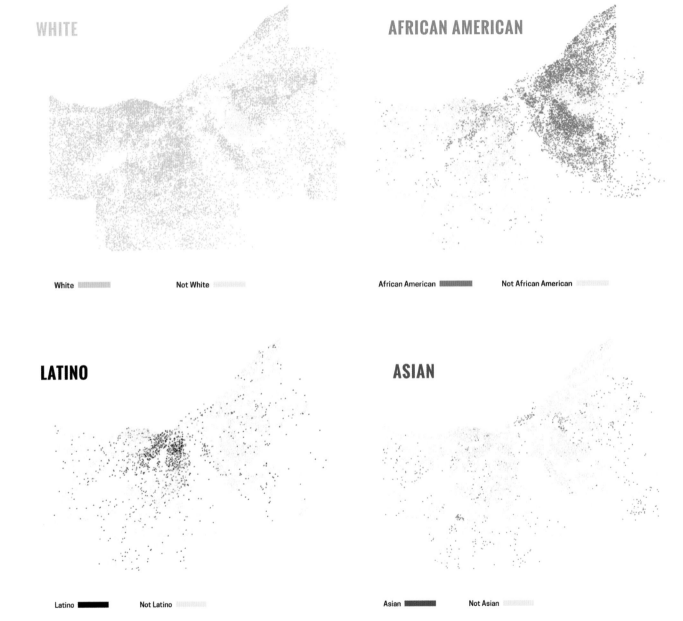

WHITE

White ▭▭▭▭▭▭   Not White ▭▭▭▭▭▭

AFRICAN AMERICAN

African American ▭▭▭▭▭▭   Not African American ▭▭▭▭▭▭

LATINO

Latino ▭▭▭▭▭▭   Not Latino ▭▭▭▭▭▭

ASIAN

Asian ▭▭▭▭▭▭   Not Asian ▭▭▭▭▭▭

According to data compiled by the American Community Survey (ACS) in 2017, the total population of Cuyahoga County is approximately 1.25 million. Of that, approximately 59 percent identify as White/Caucasian, 29 percent identify as Black/African American, 6 percent as Hispanic, 3 percent as Asian, and 3 percent as Other/Mixed. You can see the geographic distribution of these populations in the maps on the opposite page.

Within those large (and sometimes problematic) racial categorizations, a myriad of smaller ethnic identities emerge. According to the 2010 Census, the county's largest ancestral populations were German (17%), Irish (13%), Italian (9%), Polish (8%), English (6%), and Slovak (3%). Approximately 12 percent speak a language other than English at home. A little more than 7 percent were born outside the United States.

In terms of social statistics, approximately 90 percent of county residents graduated from high school, and over 32 percent hold a Bachelor's degree or higher. Forty-two percent of the population is married, and the gender split between residents is 52 percent female, 48 percent male. Eighteen percent of residents live below the poverty line, including 27 percent of children under the age of 18 and 10 percent of seniors over the age of 65. The median household income is $46,784, while the per capita income is $31,601.

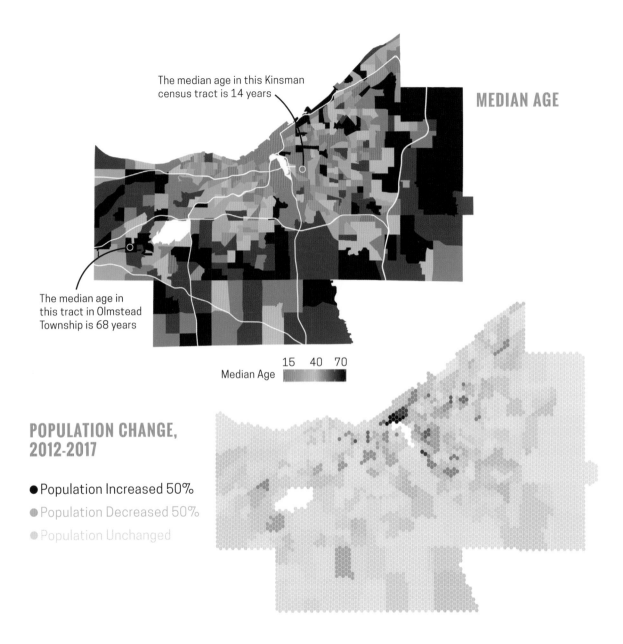

MEDIAN AGE

The median age in this Kinsman census tract is 14 years

The median age in this tract in Olmstead Township is 68 years

15   40   70
Median Age

POPULATION CHANGE, 2012-2017

● Population Increased 50%

● Population Decreased 50%

● Population Unchanged

PERCENT OF RESIDENTS IN THE SAME HOUSE AS PRIOR YEAR

Less than 75% same house 100% same house

% same house as one year ago

Together, these three maps give a sense of the movement of the population around Cuyahoga County. In general the closer you get to the city center, the younger and more mobile the population becomes. Areas with the highest rate of movement are around the largest universities in the region, Case Western Reserve University in University Circle and Baldwin-Wallace University in the southwestern suburb of Berea. Economic insecurity in low-income neighborhoods also leads to greater transiency and evictions.

Legend:
- 1910 - 1939
- **1940 - 1979**
- 1980 - 2019

Albanian
Vietnamese
Serbian
Armenian
Turkish
Azerbaijan
Native American
Polish
Slovenian
Romanian
Czech
Rusin Garden
African American
Slovak
Italian
Lithuanian
Greek
German
Ukrainian
Hungarian
Latvian
British
Syrian
Croatia
Estonian
Hebrew
Finnish
Peace Garden of the Nations
Irish
Lebanese
India
Pakistan
Ethiopian
Chinese

CULTURAL GARDENS OVER TIME

1910-2019

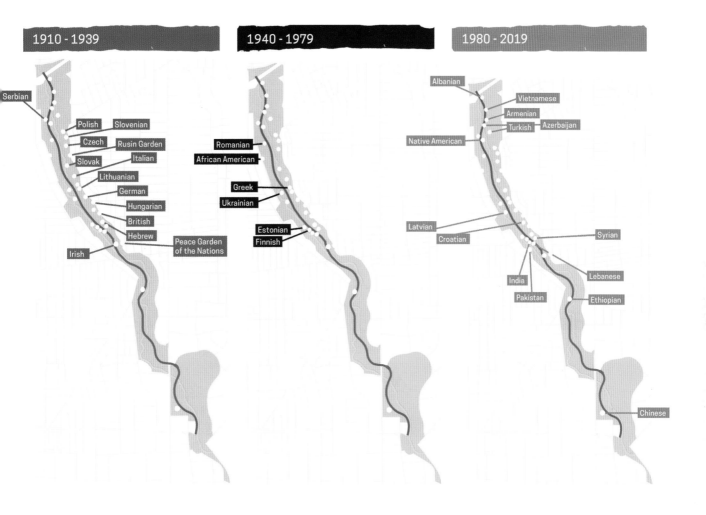

The Rockefeller Cultural Gardens, representing distinct communities throughout the city, are one of Cleveland's greatest treasures. The Cultural Gardens flank either side of the main thoroughfare that connects the busy I-90 to the heart of University Circle's museum & arts district. While that may sound like a recipe for traffic jams and stressful commutes, it is actually one of the most scenic and beautiful drives in the city.

The gardens have evolved as America's (and subsequently Cleveland's) immigrant communities have grown and changed. The years in which they were added, as you can see here, show how the ethnic makeup of the city has shifted over time. The newest planned addition is the Lebanese garden, which was announced in 2012.

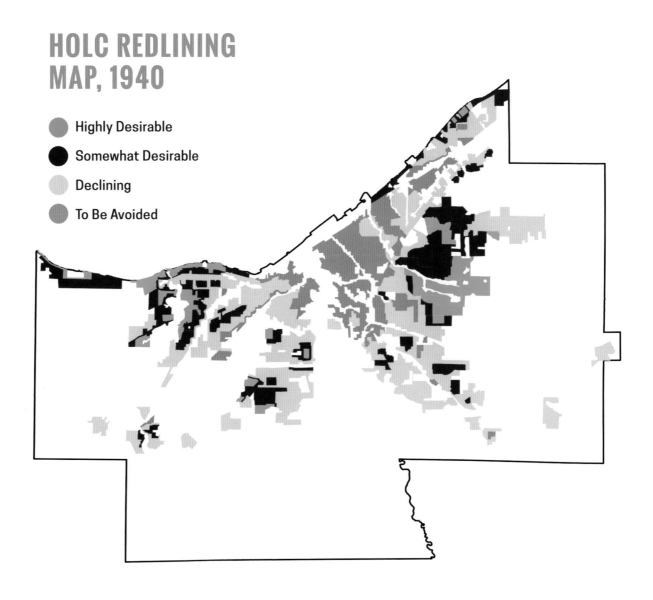

HOLC REDLINING
MAP, 1940

- Highly Desirable
- Somewhat Desirable
- Declining
- To Be Avoided

HIGH POVERTY
TRACTS IN HIGHEST POVERTY QUARTILE

LOW VEHICLE ACCESS
TRACTS IN THE LOWEST QUARTILE
FOR VEHICLE ACCESS

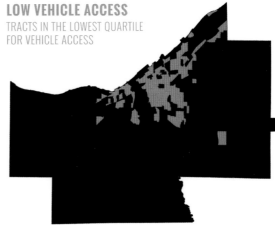

LOW INTERNET ACCESS
TRACTS IN THE LOWEST QUARTILE
FOR INTERNET ACCESS

In the 1930s, the Home Owners' Loan Corporation (HOLC) set out to evaluate mortgage-lending risk in American cities. The resulting maps codified and legitimized the racism of the day, drawing literal red lines around neighborhoods deemed high risk because of "undesirable inhabitant types." African Americans living in these areas were excluded from the mortgage market and targeted by predatory lenders, creating a cycle of insecurity and poverty.

The legacy of this bureaucratic discrimination is still in apparent in Cleveland today, as redlining boundaries line up with areas of high poverty, low vehicle access, and low internet access.

Each ● represents one foreclosed property

FORECLOSURES, 2006-2016

Like many other cities in America and around the world, Cleveland was hit hard during the so-called Great Recession triggered by the stock market crash in 2008. Unscrupulous lending practices were at the heart of the unfolding crisis, with "subprime" mortgagees—who tended to be working class and minorities—suddenly facing extreme spikes in interest rates. Many could no longer afford their payments and were forced to abandon their homes.

As you can see from this map, while much of Cuyahoga County was affected, the east side of Cleveland bore the brunt of it. For example, the ZIP code 44105, which covers Slavic Village, had more foreclosures than any other in the country. You can also clearly see how the high concentration areas here tend to mirror the redlining map on page 60, yet another sign of that policy's long lasting effects.

While foreclosures have lessened some since this height, rates have been increasing since 2016. In 2018, Cuyahoga County had the highest foreclosure rate in the state of Ohio, and saw a 77 percent increase in filings over the previous year. With a total of 1,016 filings, one in every 609 properties in the county had a foreclosure filing in 2018.

2014

2015

2016
PARTIAL YEAR

OPIOID-RELATED DEATHS

From 2014 to 2016, Ohio led the nation in opioid-related deaths. In Cuyahoga County alone, the total number of overdose deaths rose from 353 in 2014 to 666 in 2016. Of those, opioids were the cause of 214 and 557 deaths in those two years, respectively. According to a report in the *Plain Dealer*, heroin and fentanyl killed more people in Cuyahoga County in 2016 than homicides, suicides, or car crashes.

As you can see in these maps, by far the hardest hit sections are west side neighborhoods like Ohio City and Cudell, as well as suburbs such as Lakewood.

Perhaps more alarming is the diffusion of deaths over 2015 and 2016, spreading more evenly across the region as the overall numbers climbed higher.

The crisis is far from over. In 2017, the National Institute on Drug Abuse (NIDA) reported that Ohio had the second-highest rate of opioid-related deaths in the entire United States. Though overdose deaths in Cuyahoga County decreased sharply in 2018, they remain well above pre-crisis levels. HIV infection caused by intravenous drug use is also on the rise statewide.

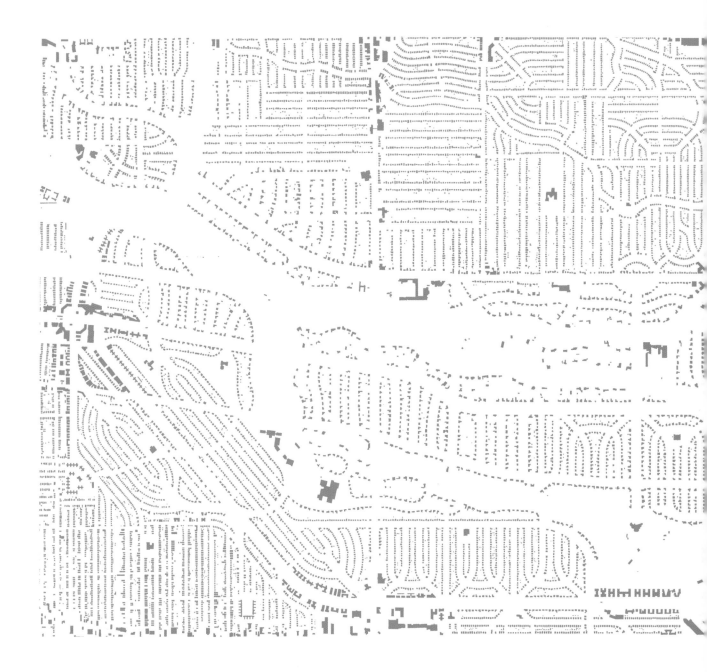

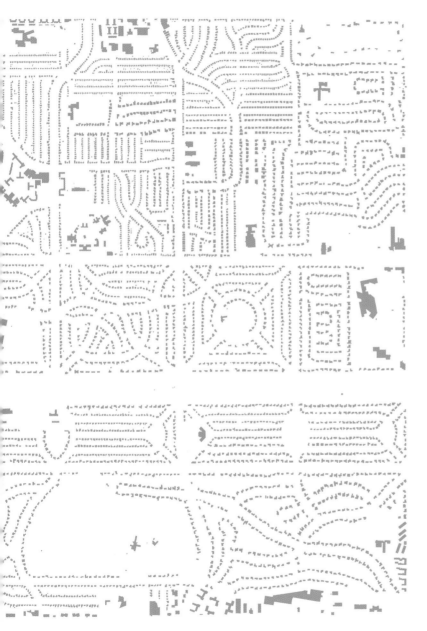

BUILDINGS IN SHAKER HEIGHTS

Shaker Heights may be Cleveland's best-known suburb. One of America's most famous planned neighborhoods, Shaker Heights today rings in the national consciousness as a town of contradictions. Its demographics include some of the wealthiest families in Northeast Ohio, living alongside some of the poorest.

The unique city planning shown here is famous among urbanists across the country. The streets are deliberately set at unusual angles to allow easy access to the Blue and Green Rapid lines, which cut through the heart of the town. Each neighborhood also has its own school nestled within the residential area, letting parents safely walk their children to class each morning. As you can see in this map, together it creates a strikingly original layout, with the beautiful Shaker Lakes as a focal point.

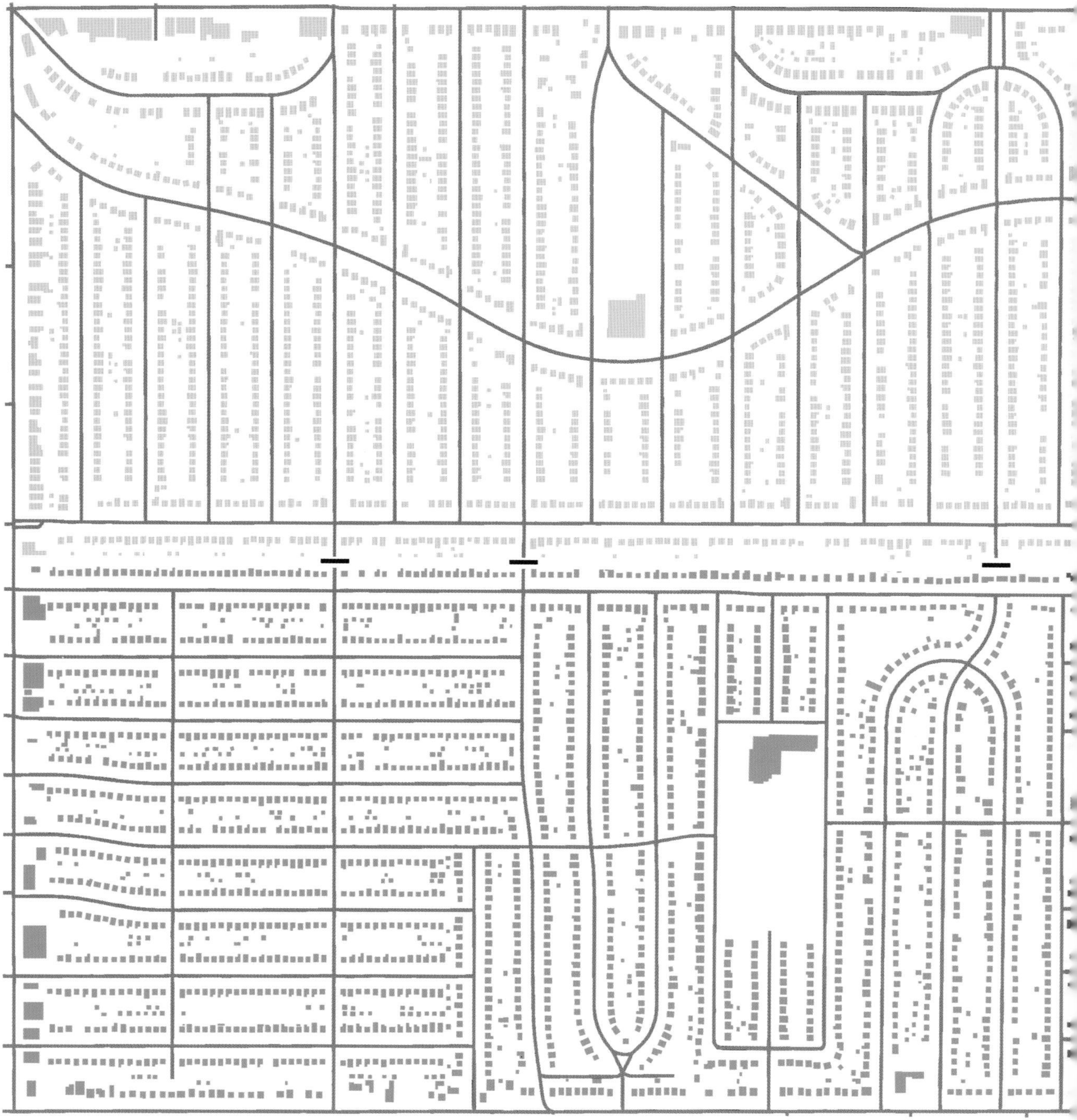

SHAKER HEIGHTS BARRICADES

One of the most controversial and defining elements of Shaker Heights are the physical barriers constructed at its border with neighboring Cleveland and Warrensville Heights. Streets that should connect simply don't, instead either looping back around to the next street over or ending abruptly in a barricade.

The barricades were first erected in 1976, when temporary traffic blockers were quietly placed where Scottsdale Boulevard intersects with Avalon and Ingleside Roads, as well as several other streets that connect Shaker Heights with the Lee-Harvard area. The stated reason was to avoid congestion on Shaker streets, but the effects—psychological and otherwise—of a physical barrier between two adjacent communities of disparate socioeconomic means are hard to ignore (or to justify).

Shaker Heights

Warrensville Heights

Cleveland

COLUMBIA PARK MOBILE HOME COMMUNITY

The Columbia Park Mobile Homes in North Olmstead offers an interesting conceptual counterpoint to Shaker Heights. Located about 15 miles from downtown Cleveland, it was conceived as a 55-and-older retirement community for those of modest means.

But unlike the standard row-by-row grid of most mobile home parks, the planners opted to make the layout feel more intentional. Like the winding streets of Shaker Heights, once inside the gates it's easy to get lost in the maze-like cul-de-sacs.

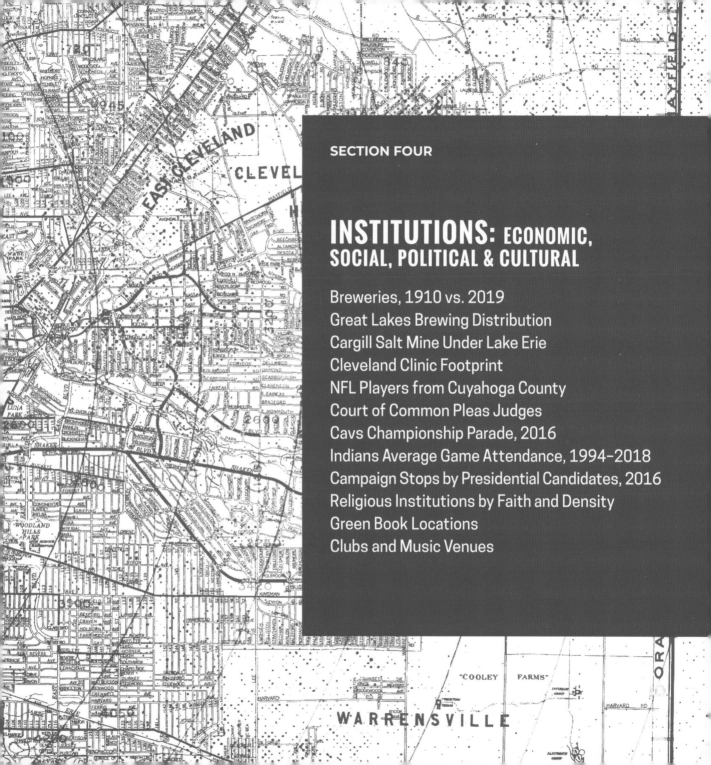

SECTION FOUR

INSTITUTIONS: ECONOMIC, SOCIAL, POLITICAL & CULTURAL

Breweries, 1910 vs. 2019
Great Lakes Brewing Distribution
Cargill Salt Mine Under Lake Erie
Cleveland Clinic Footprint
NFL Players from Cuyahoga County
Court of Common Pleas Judges
Cavs Championship Parade, 2016
Indians Average Game Attendance, 1994–2018
Campaign Stops by Presidential Candidates, 2016
Religious Institutions by Faith and Density
Green Book Locations
Clubs and Music Venues

CLEVELAND BREWERIES, 1910

Given its large Eastern European population, it's no surprise that pre-Prohibition Cleveland was awash in breweries. As you can see in the map above, they were fairly evenly distributed across downtown and the West Side, with clusters in St Clair/Superior, the Flats, and Ohio City.

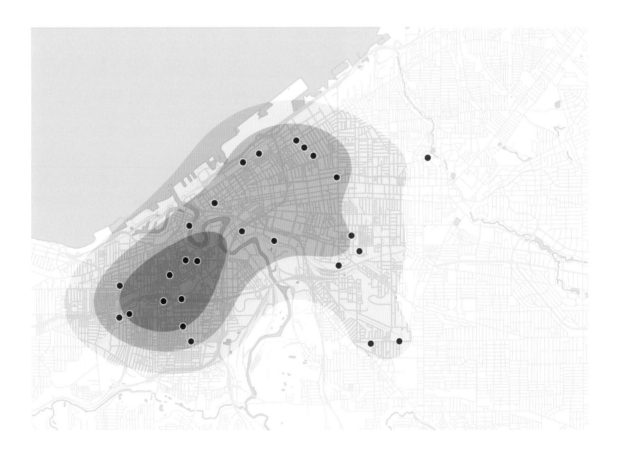

CLEVELAND BREWERIES, 2019

Cleveland's brewery scene sprung to life again starting with the craft beer boom in the 1990s. Today, Cleveland is no different from the rest of America—find a hipster enclave, you will find a brewery nearby. Ohio City is uncontested in its dominance of the Cleveland beer market right now. In addition to stalwart Great Lakes Brewing Company, new West Side breweries include Saucy Brew Works, Market Garden, Bookhouse, Hansa, Forest City, Brick & Barrel, and Platform.

Cleveland beer isn't just for locals, though. The aforementioned Great Lakes Brewing Company ships its offerings, including the immensely popular Christmas Ale and Burning River Pale Ale, as far north as Duluth, as far east as Albany, and as far south as Wilmington, NC.

GREAT LAKES BREWING COMPANY DISTRIBUTION ROUTES

CARGILL SALT MINE UNDER LAKE ERIE

You'd be forgiven for not knowing about the colossal underground salt mine that surrounds the mouth of the Cuyahoga River. Stretching for nearly five miles and roughly 1,700 feet below the surface, the Cargill-run mine produces millions of tons of rock salt each year. Conveniently located under a major shipping port, salt from the mine is shipped throughout the Great Lakes and as far east as Massachusetts.

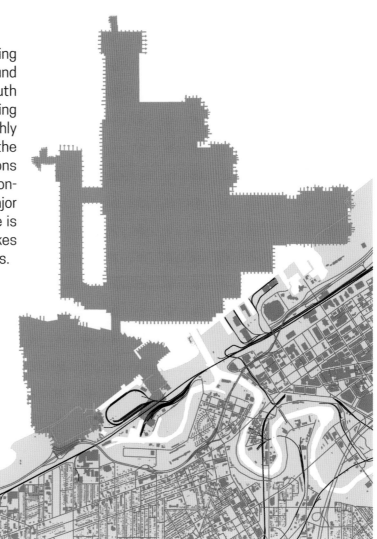

CLEVELAND CLINIC, THE EARLY YEARS

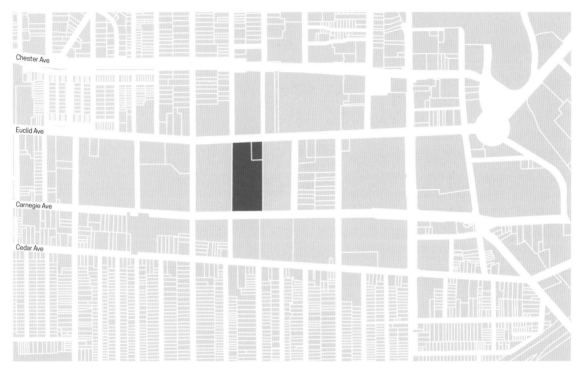

Chester Ave

Euclid Ave

Carnegie Ave

Cedar Ave

The Cleveland Clinic occupies a massive footprint on the city's east side. Founded in 1921, by 1930 the Clinic had already taken over an entire city block. Since then, the hospital has overtaken blocks and blocks of real estate within the neighborhoods of Hough and Fairfax, among others.

CLEVELAND CLINIC, TODAY

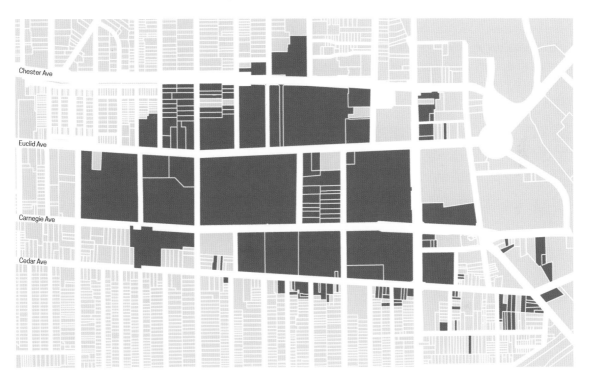

There is little doubt of the benefits the Cleveland Clinic has brought to the world—the cancer research alone has saved millions—but questions have been raised about the Clinic being headquartered in the heart of an underprivileged neighborhood that is not serviced by its staff of world-class professionals. While the Clinic regularly intakes presidents and kings from around the world, local neighbors without the means cannot access its services. Additionally, what this map doesn't show are the dozens of satellite outposts, offices, and full-fledged hospitals dotting the suburban landscape.

NFL PLAYERS FROM CUYAHOGA COUNTY

High school football in Northeast Ohio is serious business. Local schools recruit from around the city and county, and Cleveland-area coaches are known for preparing athletes for the next level. Power programs like Glenville, Benedictine, Cathedral Latin, and Saint Ignatius currently have the most former players in the NFL.

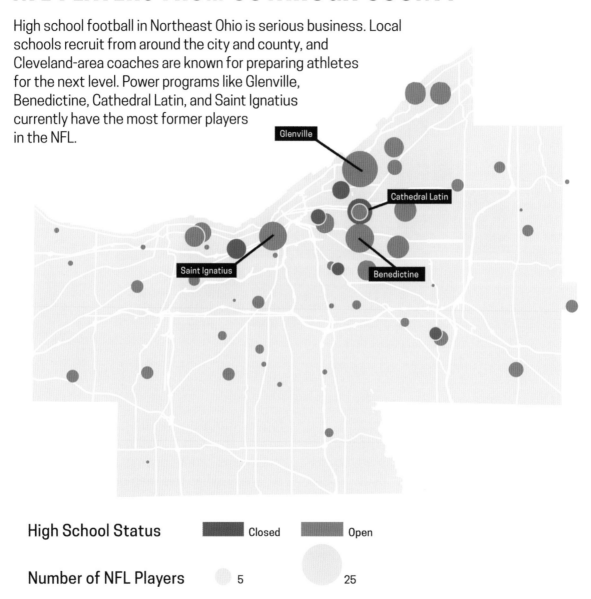

High School Status   Closed   Open

Number of NFL Players   5   25

COURT OF COMMON PLEAS JUDGES BY HIGH SCHOOL

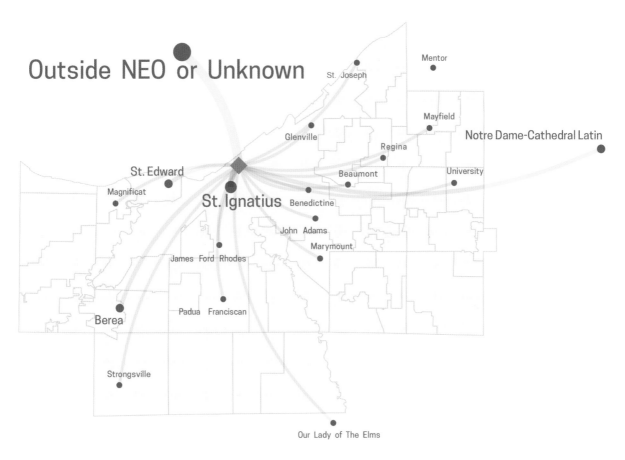

Outside NEO or Unknown

St. Joseph

Mentor

Mayfield

Glenville

Regina

Notre Dame-Cathedral Latin

St. Edward

Beaumont

University

Magnificat

St. Ignatius

Benedictine

John Adams

Marymount

James Ford Rhodes

Berea

Padua   Franciscan

Strongsville

Our Lady of The Elms

Interestingly, all four schools also have a solid record of turning out judges elected to serve on the Cuyahoga County Court of Common Pleas. Other star legal preparatory programs include Berea, Notre Dame-Cathedral Catholic, and St. Edward.

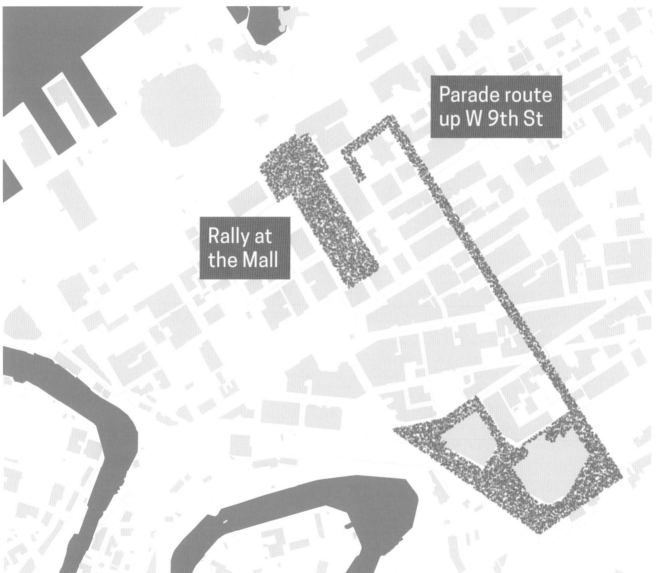

Each ● = 100 People

Parade route
up W 9th St

Rally at
the Mall

CAVS 2016 CHAMPIONSHIP PARADE AND RALLY

There were two types of Clevelanders the night of the Cavaliers victory over the Golden State Warriors for the national championship in June 2016: those who believed it was destiny, and those who thought it was a dream. The Cavs had never won an NBA title before and had played in the Finals only twice before—2007 and 2015, both teams led by local hero LeBron James. They trailed the series three games to one after Game 4, but rallied to win the next three games and claim a tearful victory.

It wasn't just a victory for the Cavs, though. As any good Clevelander knows, none of the city's big three professional teams had won a national championship in any sport since the 1940s, despite coming tantalizingly close every few years. The long drought was such a local obsession that it became a national story (or a national joke, depending on your point of view). In May 2016, ESPN aired a documentary in its "30 for 30" series titled *Believeland*, featuring famous Northeast Ohio residents such as Andy Borowitz and Scott Raab discussing all their years of sports disappointment and despair. The ending of that film had to be edited only a few short weeks later.

After the Cavs triumph, hundreds of area businesses gave their employees time off to celebrate this once-in-a-lifetime event, and an estimated 1.3 million fans flooded downtown to greet the conquering heroes. The parade started outside what was then known as Quicken Loans Arena, then proceeded slowly up West 9th Street, culminating in a rally on the Convention Center Mall.

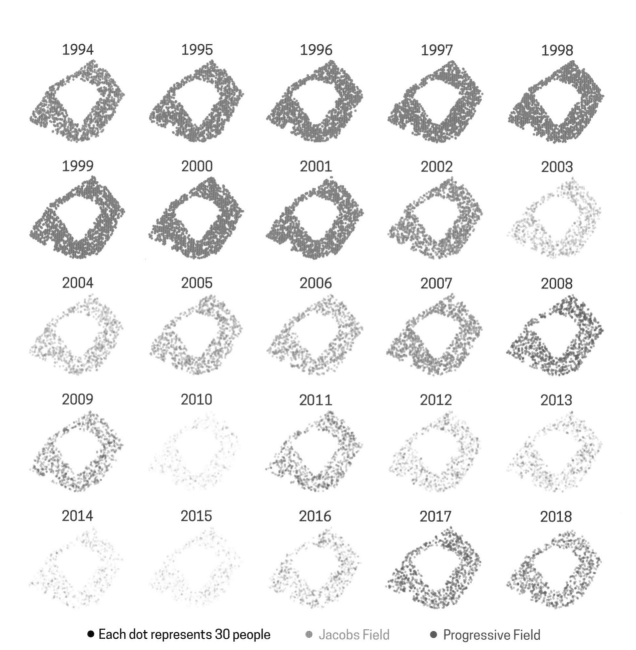

1994	1995	1996	1997	1998
1999	2000	2001	2002	2003
2004	2005	2006	2007	2008
2009	2010	2011	2012	2013
2014	2015	2016	2017	2018

● Each dot represents 30 people   ● Jacobs Field   ● Progressive Field

CLEVELAND INDIANS AVERAGE GAME ATTENDANCE

The Indians are undeniably a big deal in Cleveland. Founded in Grand Rapids, Michigan in 1894, the Tribe has called Cleveland home since 1901, when they were called the Bluebirds. After a brief stint as the Napoleons, in 1915 the team changed their name to Indians, supposedly in recognition of a Native American player on the old Cleveland Spiders team named Louis Sockalexis. (Check out Brad Ricca's excellent essay "The Secret History of Chief Wahoo" in *Belt Magazine* for more on this rather dubious origin story.)

Controversial name and logo aside, rooting for the Indians is a cherished summer ritual here. No one wants to admit they are a fairweather fan, but the pattern of attendance at games since the opening of Jacobs Field (affectionately dubbed "the Jake") in 1994 seems to suggest that many Tribe fans are just that. Clevelanders rightly look back fondly at the glory days of Albert Bell, Sandy Alomar, and Kenny Lofton, and for five years running from 1995 to 1999 the Indians made the playoffs and fans came out in droves.

The "rebuilding" years of 2003 to 2006 saw a sharp dip in attendance, and the numbers vacillated back and forth after the stadium was renamed for local insurance giant Progressive. Even in 2016, which saw the Indians make the World Series for the first time in two decades, attendance never climbed back to the heights of the early days of the Jake.

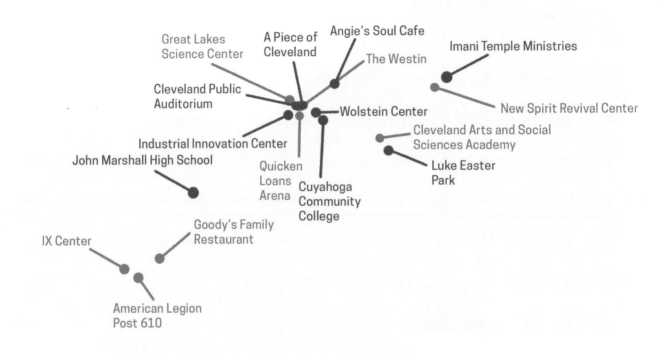

Great Lakes Science Center

A Piece of Cleveland

Angie's Soul Cafe

Imani Temple Ministries

The Westin

Cleveland Public Auditorium

Wolstein Center

New Spirit Revival Center

Industrial Innovation Center

Cleveland Arts and Social Sciences Academy

John Marshall High School

Quicken Loans Arena

Cuyahoga Community College

Luke Easter Park

Goody's Family Restaurant

IX Center

American Legion Post 610

DONALD TRUMP **HILLARY CLINTON**

PRESIDENTIAL CAMPAIGN STOPS, 2016

The presidential election of 2016 was perhaps one of the most consequential (and controversial) in American history, and Cleveland was right at the center of it. As one of the major population centers in a deep purple, double-digit electoral vote swing state, Cuyahoga County was visited countless times by both Democratic nominee Hillary Clinton and Republican Donald Trump, who received his nomination at the Republican National Convention in Cleveland that summer.

Each candidate's choice of venues says a lot about their respective constituencies—or at least how each campaign viewed their base of support. On September 5, Donald Trump made a surprise appearance at the American Legion outpost in Brook Park, where he gladhanded with the Teamsters and UAW representatives as well as leaders from the Ohio Police Benevolent Association and the Cleveland Firefighters Union. Afterward he stopped at the nearby Goody's Family Restaurant, a local favorite.

Clinton, meanwhile, made her own surprise visit on Halloween, having lunch with Congresswoman Marcia Fudge at Angie's Soul Café on East 34th & St. Clair. In July, Clinton and her running mate Tim Kaine had attended services at Imani Temple Ministries in Cleveland Heights, while Trump visited the New Spirit Revival Center just down the street.

DENSITY OF RELIGIOUS INSTITUTIONS IN CUYAHOGA COUNTY

Each ● represents one institution

RELIGIOUS INSTITUTIONS BY FAITH

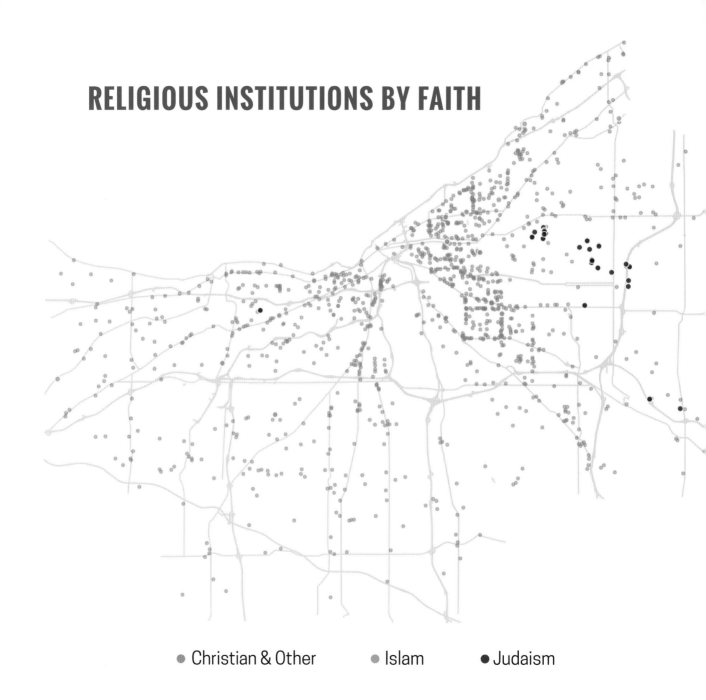

● Christian & Other   ● Islam   ●Judaism

CHURCHES IN THE CENTRAL NEIGHBORHOOD

Certain communities throughout the city are known for their affiliation with a particular faith. The near east side neighborhoods of Hough, Fairfax, and, in particular, Central, are known for an abundance of Christian churches with fervent congregations. There are at least 15 separate operational churches within a two-square-mile section of Central between East 55th Street and East 71st Street.

Similarly, the east side suburbs of Cleveland Heights, Shaker Heights, and Beachwood are home to the vast majority of the city's synagogues. No single neighborhood or area holds a disproportionate number of mosques, however.

Quincy Ave

Woodland Ave

Kinsman Rd

Other Property

Relgious Institutions

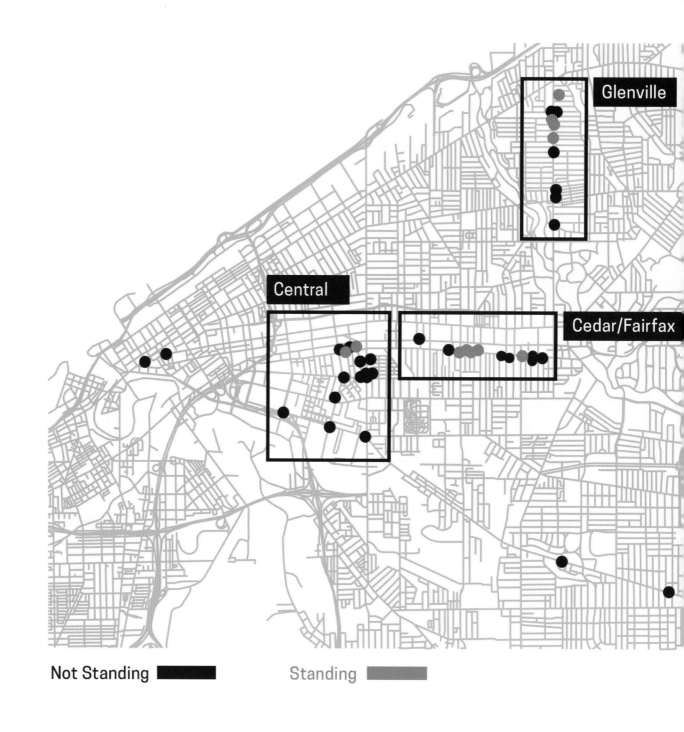

Glenville

Central

Cedar/Fairfax

Not Standing ▮▮▮▮▮   Standing ▮▮▮▮▮

CLEVELAND LOCATIONS IN
THE GREEN BOOK

The Negro Motorist Green Book was published yearly between 1936 and 1966. It was launched during the height of Southern Jim Crow laws to help African Americans avoid discrimination and worse while driving in the United States, particularly those taking a road trip or vacation. The guidebook, named after its founder, Victor Hugo Green, identified places African Americans would feel welcome. Many of these were African American–owned. Drivers visiting Cleveland using the *Green Book* were advised as to which gas stations, restaurants, night clubs, hotels, drug stores, and hair salons would make for good stops. Visitors were directed to neighborhoods that were then—and remain today—primarily African American: Glenville, Cedar/Fairfax, and Central.

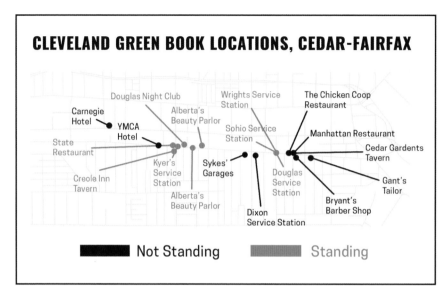

CLEVELAND GREEN BOOK LOCATIONS, CEDAR-FAIRFAX

Douglas Night Club

Wrights Service Station

The Chicken Coop Restaurant

Carnegie Hotel

Alberta's Beauty Parlor

YMCA Hotel

Manhattan Restaurant

Sohio Service Station

State Restaurant

Cedar Gardents Tavern

Kyer's Service Station

Sykes' Garages

Douglas Service Station

Gant's Tailor

Creole Inn Tavern

Alberta's Beauty Parlor

Bryant's Barber Shop

Dixon Service Station

■■■■ Not Standing   ■■■■ Standing

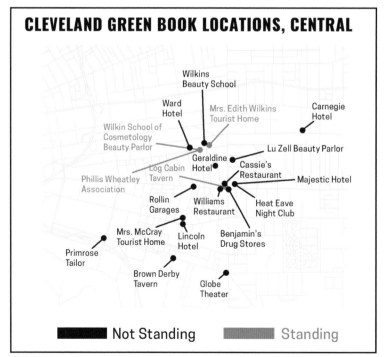

CLEVELAND GREEN BOOK LOCATIONS, CENTRAL

Wilkins Beauty School

Ward Hotel

Mrs. Edith Wilkins Tourist Home

Carnegie Hotel

Wilkin School of Cosmetology Beauty Parlor

Lu Zell Beauty Parlor

Geraldine Hotel

Cassie's Restaurant

Log Cabin Tavern

Majestic Hotel

Phillis Wheatley Association

Rollin Garages

Williams Restaurant

Heat Eave Night Club

Mrs. McCray Tourist Home

Lincoln Hotel

Benjamin's Drug Stores

Primrose Tailor

Brown Derby Tavern

Globe Theater

■■■■ Not Standing   ■■■■ Standing

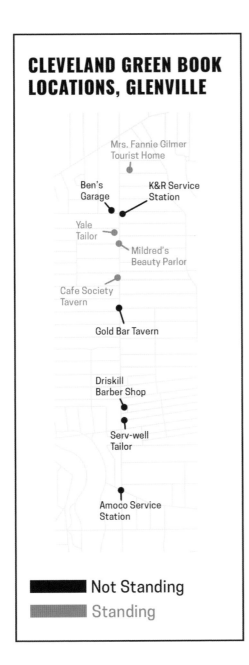

CLEVELAND GREEN BOOK LOCATIONS, GLENVILLE

Mrs. Fannie Gilmer
Tourist Home

Ben's
Garage

K&R Service
Station

Yale
Tailor

Mildred's
Beauty Parlor

Cafe Society
Tavern

Gold Bar Tavern

Driskill
Barber Shop

Serv-well
Tailor

Amoco Service
Station

■■■ Not Standing
■■■ Standing

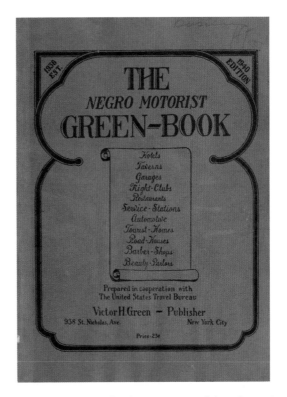

1856 EST.

1940 EDITION

THE
NEGRO MOTORIST
GREEN-BOOK

Hotels
Taverns
Garages
Night-Clubs
Restaurants
Service-Stations
Automotive
Tourist-Homes
Road-Houses
Barber-Shops
Beauty-Parlors

Prepared in cooperation with
The United States Travel Bureau

Victor H. Green — Publisher
958 St. Nicholas Ave.   New York City

Price 25¢

Nearly all of these neighborhood businesses have since closed, and most of the buildings that housed them are no longer standing, either. But some locations remain, such as the site of the Phillis Wheatley Association in Central.

ESSENTIAL CLEVELAND MUSIC VENUES
PAST AND PRESENT

JAZZ VENUES
ROCK VENUES
POLKA VENUES

JAZZ VENUES

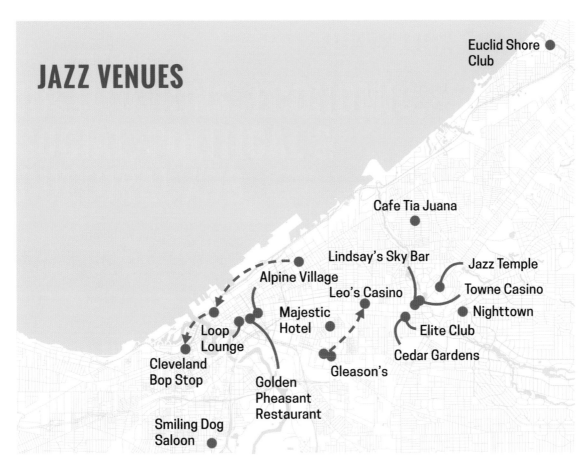

Euclid Shore Club

Cafe Tia Juana

Lindsay's Sky Bar

Alpine Village

Jazz Temple

Leo's Casino

Towne Casino

Majestic Hotel

Nighttown

Loop Lounge

Elite Club

Cleveland Bop Stop

Cedar Gardens

Golden Pheasant Restaurant

Gleason's

Smiling Dog Saloon

Perhaps the first truly American popular music, jazz has been a part of the Cleveland concert scene from its earliest days. As musicians from New Orleans moved north during the Great Migration, Cleveland's status as a hub for the best acts continued to grow. Venues such as Cafe Tia Juana, Loop Lounge, and Gleason's welcomed such luminaries as Dizzy Gillespie and Charles Mingus during the 1950s. While most of the best venues closed in the 1970s, a few prominent ones, such as Nighttown in Cleveland Heights, still carry the torch.

ROCK AND ROLL VENUES

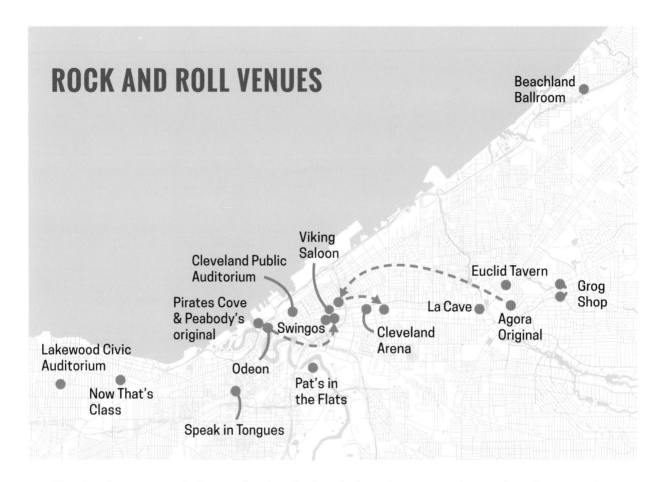

Cleveland's status as the home of rock and roll music may still be the subject of dispute, but its rock credentials are beyond reproach. The Moondog Coronation Ball, considered by many to be the first rock concert in history, was held at Cleveland Arena on March 21, 1952. The Beatles played to a packed house at the Public Auditorium in 1964. La Cave hosted shows by folk stars Simon & Garfunkel and Arlo Guthrie before becoming the preferred venue for the Velvet Underground. When David Bowie toured America for the first time, he started in Cleveland. The city's array of rock venues also nurtured homegrown talent, such as protopunk pioneers Rocket from the Tombs in the 1970s, future Nine Inch Nails frontman Trent Reznor in the 1980s, and the alt-metal act Mushroomhead in the 1990s.

POLKA VENUES

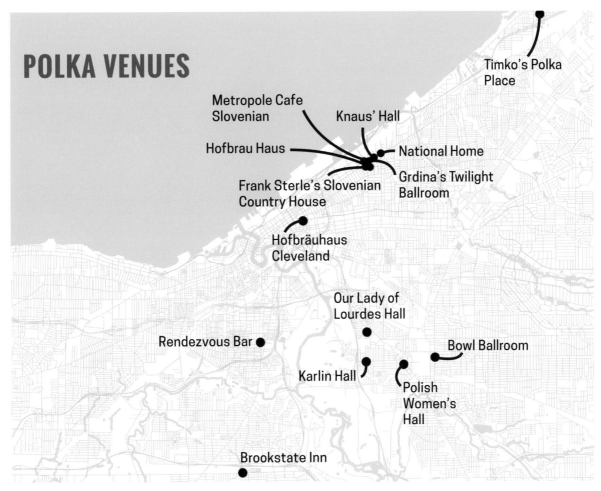

Timko's Polka Place

Metropole Cafe Slovenian

Knaus' Hall

Hofbrau Haus

National Home

Grdina's Twilight Ballroom

Frank Sterle's Slovenian Country House

Hofbräuhaus Cleveland

Our Lady of Lourdes Hall

Rendezvous Bar

Bowl Ballroom

Karlin Hall

Polish Women's Hall

Brookstate Inn

With its large Eastern European population, Cleveland also has a rich history of polka. Cleveland-style polka is even considered its own subgenre, drawing on the Slovenian tradition and always featuring the accordion. Many of the city's most prominent polka venues are clustered near the intersection of St. Clair Avenue and East 55th Street, a longtime Slovenian stronghold. Perhaps the most well-known polka star is Collinwood native Frankie Yankovic, whose recording of the song "Just Because" went platinum in 1947. The National Cleveland-Style Polka Hall of Fame is located in Euclid, near Yankovic's old neighborhood.

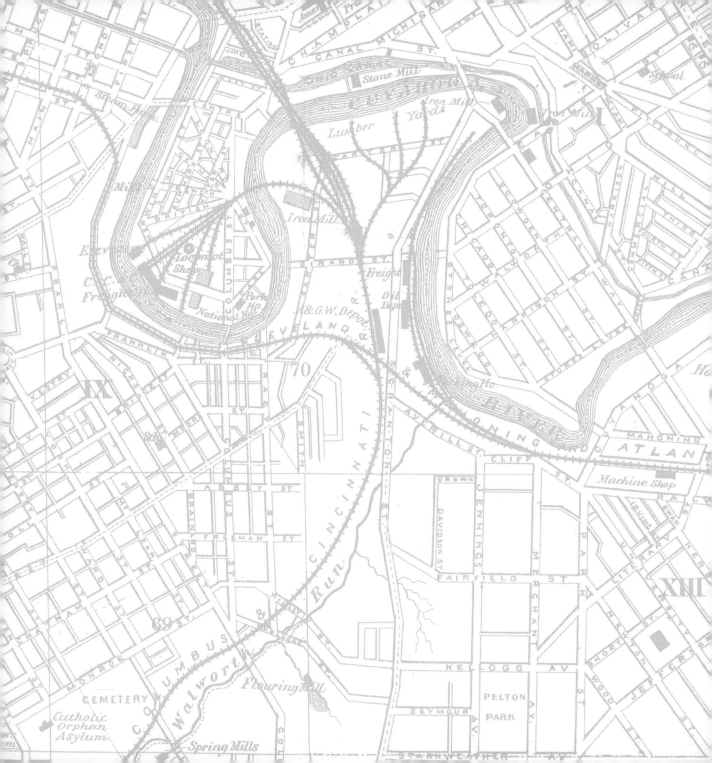

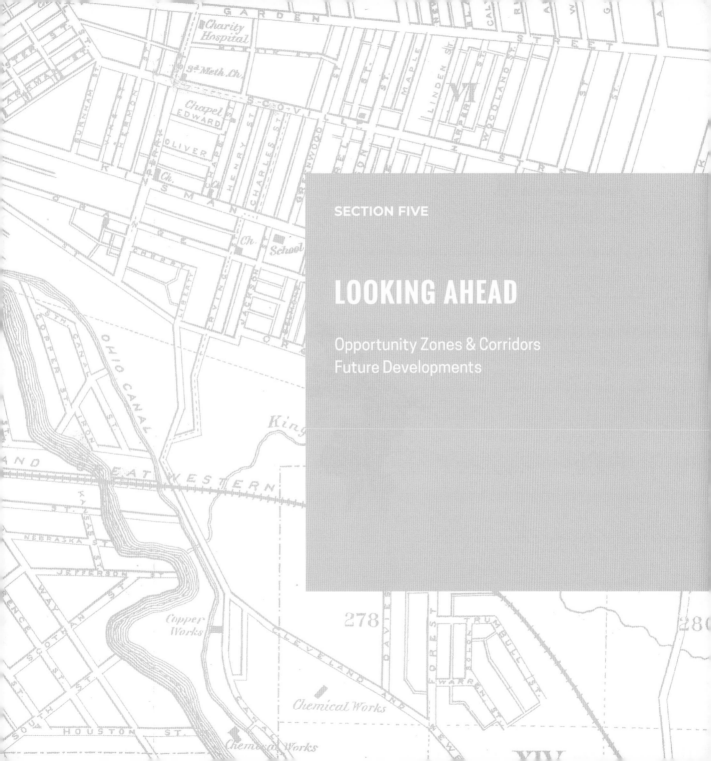

LOOKING AHEAD

Opportunity Zones & Corridors
Future Developments

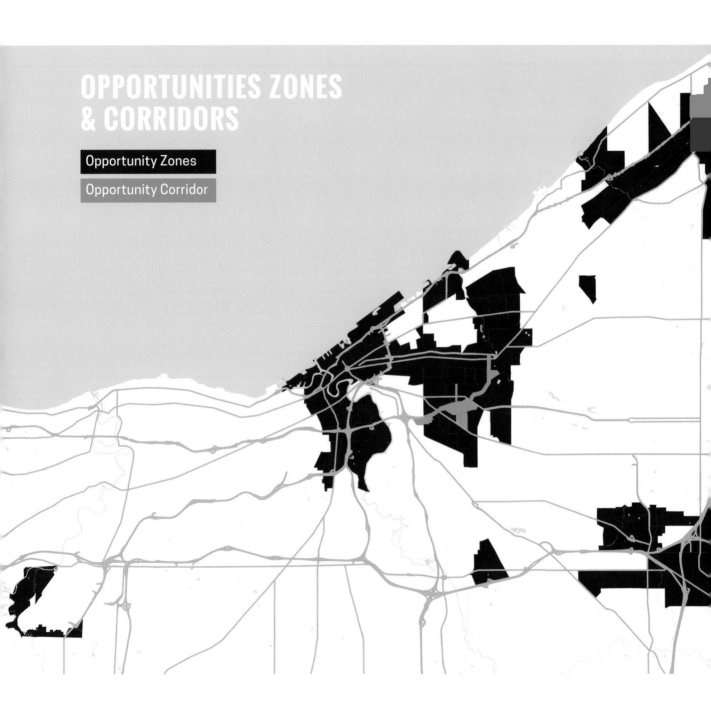

OPPORTUNITIES ZONES & CORRIDORS

Opportunity Zones

Opportunity Corridor

"Opportunity" appears to be the buzzword of current development initiatives throughout Cleveland. The Tax Cuts and Jobs Act, passed by the Republican-controlled Congress in 2017, designated certain low-income census tracts throughout the country as so-called Opportunity Zones, which creates tax incentives for certain types of investments in those areas. However, the benefits of this program are not limited solely to "low-income" areas. Downtown, for instance, is considered an Opportunity Zone. So are all of Ohio City and Tremont. Also, use of census tracts leads to somewhat arbitrary boundaries for incentivized areas; the northeast and southwest corners of the intersection of Superior Ave & East 55th Street fall under the program, for example, while the northwest and southeast corners do not.

A separate local program also borrows the language of opportunity. The "Opportunity Corridor" is a $300 million road-building project on the city's east side. Phases I and II of the project, completed in 2017 and 2018 respectively, involved revitalizing portions of East 105th Street around the Cleveland Clinic and creating a connection between Norman Avenue and East 93rd Street. Phase III is designed to improve automobile access from the I-490 interchange through the Kinsman and Buckeye-Shaker neighborhoods, often dubbed the "Forgotten Triangle." The new road will be a four-lane, tree-lined boulevard, and its path requires the destruction of dozens of existing homes and commercial buildings.

These are only a few of the many development initiatives planned for the region in the coming years. The map on the next page shows several others, including the Shaker Square revitalization and the Red Line Greenway. But future maps of Cleveland have not yet been set in stone. Far from it. You can help shape the way these projects and others unfold by getting involved with community organizations and development corporations, attending public hearings and city council meetings, and, most importantly, voting.

MAJOR PROPOSED DEVELOPMENT SITES ACROSS CLEVELAND

Red Line
Greenway

akefront

Metrohealth

Shaker
Square

Opportunity
Corridor

SOURCES

p. 20-23: Historical facts and information sourced from the Encyclopedia of Cleveland History (case.edu/ech) and the US Census Bureau (census.gov). The data were digitized by Will Skora from an unnamed 1968 map and the 1941 Volkmann map held by the Cleveland Public Library. The data are available here: https://github.com/skorasaurus/cleboundaries

p. 24-25: The tree canopy data are from the 2011 National Land Cover Database produced by the USGS. The data were aggregated and averaged across a grid of hexagons to form the final map.

p. 26-27: These maps are derived from the USGS DEM files downloaded from the Ohio Geographically Referenced Information Program. The DEM raster tiles were first converted to contour files and then stitched together to create the final dataset.

p. 28-29: Hydrography data from Cuyahoga County Open Data. Extended river data from OpenStreetMap contributors. Downloaded from overpass-turbo.eu under ODbL.

p. 30: 2017 hydrography and FEMA flood data from Cuyahoga County Open Data.

p. 31: Data from NOAA's Great Lakes Environmental Research Laboratory.

p. 32: Spatial data from the Metroparks' Github page, accessed under CC0 1.0. The raw shapes were converted into a grid of hexagons for mapping.

p. 33: Attendance data from the Cleveland Metroparks "2015 Enhanced Visitation Evaluation" available on the Metroparks' website. Visits are measures in a unit called "Visitor Occasions", which counts the number of people entering a Metroparks reservation on vehicle, foot, or bicycle for any reason.

p. 36-37: Bridge data from OpenStreetMap contributors. Downloaded from overpass-turbo.eu under ODbL. Road, rivers, and rails from Cuyahoga County Open Data

p. 38-41: Data from Cuyahoga County Open Data.

p. 42: 2018 data from the Ohio Department of Public Safety.

p. 43: Data from Cuyahoga County Open Data.

p. 44-45: Data from Cuyahoga County Open Data. Map shows all parcels with a class description of "Parking" or "Commercial Garage" as of March 2017.

p. 46-47: Historical data traced from map in the 1901 McGraw Electric Railway Manual. Current data on fixed rail commuter lines from the NOACA GIS Portal. Historical facts and information provided by the GCRTA (riderta.com) and the Encyclopedia of Cleveland History (case.edu/ech).

p. 48: Library data from OpenStreetMap contributors. Downloaded from overpass-turbo.eu under ODbL. Cross referenced against addresses available on CPL's website. Theater data collected manually starting with the list available on the Cuyahoga County Visitors website and adding other locations identified by community and via Google.

p. 49: Supermarket data from OpenStreetMap contributors. Downloaded from overpass-turbo.eu under ODbL. Farmers market data from cleveland.com's 2018 list of Northeast Ohio Farmers markets.

p. 52-55: Race and ethnicity estimates from the 2017 five-year American Community Survey. Each dot represents 50 people. Thanks to Christine Zhang for her comprehensive work on population dotmaps.

p. 56-57: Population change from the 2012 to the 2017. Data from the five-year American Community Survey. Median age estimates from the 2017 five-year American Community Survey. The color scale is centered on 40, the median age for all of Cuyahoga County in 2017. Percent of population in the same house as last year from the 2017 five-year American Community Survey. The color scale is centered on 84%, the median percentage for all tracts in Cuyahoga County.

p. 58-59: Cultural Gardens data from the Cleveland Cultural Gardens Federation, updated by in-person visits to the gardens.

p. 60: Redlining map from the University of Richmond's Digital Scholarship Lab used under CC-BY-NC-SA license.

p. 61: Percent of population with income below poverty level from the 2017 five-year American Community Survey. Highest poverty quartile is 34% or more of the population in poverty. Percent of households without access to a vehicle from the 2017 five-year American Community Survey. Map shows tracts with where 25% or more of households don't have access to a vehicle. Percent of households without internet access from the 2017 five-year American Community Survey. Maps shows tracts with 30% or more households without access to the Internet.

p. 62-63: Foreclosure filings in Cuyahoga County from 2006-2016. Data from Cuyahoga County Open Data.

p. 64-65: Deaths involving opioid (heroin, fentanyl, oxycodone, etc.) from January 2014 to March 2016 as ruled by the Cuyahoga County Medical Examiner.

p. 66-67: 2018 building footprint data from Microsoft. Licensed under ODbL.

p. 68-69: 2018 building footprint data from Microsoft. Licensed under ODbL.

p. 70-71: 2018 building footprint data from Microsoft. Licensed under ODbL.

p. 74: Breweries and addresses from the 1910 Cleveland City Directory.

p. 75: Breweries and addresses from Beer Advocate (beeradvocate.com) or the Brewers Association (brewersassociation.org).

p. 76: Cities collected from the list of distributors on Great Lakes Brewing Company's website (greatlakesbrewing.com). Routes generated by Google's Directions API.

p. 77: Mine boundary as of 2003. Traced from Cargill map held in the Cleveland Public Library's map collection. Thanks to Kira Tachovsky for research assistance.

p. 78: 1930 building boundaries determined by looking at historical postcards held at the Michael Schwartz Library at Cleveland State University.

p. 79: Parcels owned by the Cleveland Clinic or an affiliate in Cuyahoga County tax records as of May 2019.

p. 80: Data from pro-football-reference.com.

p. 81: Data collected from the Cuyahoga County Court of Common Pleas website and media reports. Thanks to Kira Tachovsky for research assistance.

p. 82-83: Parade route from Cleveland Cavaliers website (nba.com/cavaliers). Attendance estimate reported via ESPN and other media outlets.

p. 84-85: Attendance data from Baseball Almanac.

p. 86-87: Data collected from p2016.org and verified by media reports.

p. 88-89: Religious institutions include houses of worship, religious cemeteries, and religious schools. Data from Cuyahoga County Land Use records as of February 2019.

p. 90: Synagogue locations collected from accessjewishcleveland.org and mosque locations collected from google.com

p. 91: Data from Cuyahoga County Land Use records as of February 2019.

p. 92-95: Address data collected from Green Books held by the New York Public Library's Schomburg Center for Research in Black Culture.

p. 97: Venues and addresses sourced from Chapter 12 of Joe Mosbrook's book *Cleveland Jazz History*

p. 98: Rock and roll venues crowdsourced from local musicians and historians. Special thanks to Daniel Goldmark and the Terrell family for their input.

p. 99: Venues and addresses sourced from the Polka page of Case Western Reserve's Encyclopedia of Cleveland History (case.edu/ech) by Joseph Valencic. Augmented by interviews with Evan's polka dancing family.

p. 102-103: Opportunity Zones data from the US Department of the Treasury's Community Development Financial Institutions Fund. Opportunity Corridor data traced from City of Cleveland maps.

p. 104-105: Maps collected from articles in cleveland.com and Crain's Cleveland (crainscleveland.com) over 2018 and 2019. Thanks to Kira Tachovsky for research assistance.

ABOUT THE CONTRIBUTORS

Dan Crissman is the associate publisher of Belt and the author of *Brewing Everything: How to Make Your Own Beer, Cider, Mead, Sake, and Other Fermented Beverages*. He lives in Cleveland.

Evan Tachovsky is a cartographer and data scientist currently working in New York City. Born and raised in Bedford, Ohio, he makes it back to Northeast Ohio as often as he can.

David Wilson is an illustrator whose work has appeared in *The Atlantic, New York Magazine, The Boston Globe*, and many more. He lives in Stow, Ohio with his wife and two daughters.